© 2017, 2015, 2013, 2008, 2007, 2005 by YouthLight, Inc.
Chapin, SC 29036

All rights reserved.
Permission is given for individuals to reproduce the activities and worksheet section in this book.
Reproduction of any other material is strictly prohibited.

Cover Design and Layout by Diane Florence
Project Editing by Susan Bowman

ISBN
978-1-59850-000-4

Library of Congress Number
2005927219

10 9 8 7
Printed in the United States

Table of Contents

Dedication 4
About the Author 5

Introduction
How to Use this Book 6
Group Options 8
Relational Aggression 10
The American School Counselor Association National Standards 12
Parent/Guardian Consent Form 15
Journaling 16

Lesson 1 – Salvaging Sisterhood
Declarations to Myself 17
Salvaging Sisterhood 21
Salvaging Sisterhood Pre-Group Survey 23
Salvaging Sisterhood Group Rules 24

Lesson 2 – Girl World
The Ties that Bind Us 25
The Ties that Bind Us Questions 27
Sisterhood Rocks 30
T.G.I.F.! 32
Sisterhood Style 33
Sisterhood Style Quiz 35
Illustrating Us 37

Lesson 3 – Friends
Our Friendship 39
A True Friend 41
Am I a Good Friend? 42
It's All About Me 47
So, You Think You Know Me? 49
Examining Friendships 50

Lesson 4 – Being Mean
Oh No She Did Not 52
Oh No She Did Not Worksheet 54
Sticks and Stones 55
The Chain of Compliments 57
Constructive vs. Destructive Criticism 58
Sugar & Spice, and Everything Nice 59
If You Don't Have Anything Nice to Say 61

© YouthLight, Inc.

Table of Contents
continued

Lesson 5 – Girl Talk
Did You Hear About.. 63
Digital Gossip 65
What's my Reputation? 67
What's my Reputation? Worksheet 69
Whatever! 70
Am I Jealous? 72
Dealing with Jealousy 74

Lesson 6 – Empathy
I'm Sorry, So Sorry! 77
The 5A Way to Make Everything OK 79
But I Really Do Feel Bad! 80
Guess How I am Feeling? 82
Spreading Sunshine 83
Spreading Sunshine Cards 85

Lesson 7 – Communication & Confrontation
Say What? 86
I Messages 88
Listen to Me! 89
Problem Solving 91
Problem Solving Worksheet 93
An Agreement to Disagree 95

Lesson 8 – Sisters Forever!
Sisters Forever 96
Dear Salvaging Sisterhood Friendship Expert 98
Friendship First Aid 101
Friendship First Aid Kit 103
Salvaging Sisterhood Contract 104
Salvaging Sisterhood Group Evaluation 105
Salvaging Sisterhood Post-Group Survey 106
Salvaging Sisterhood Certificate 107

Conclusion
Letter to Parents/Guardian 108
Salvaging Sisterhood Follow up Questionnaire 109
Publications about Relational Aggression/Bullying 110
References 112
Helpful Websites About Relational Aggression/Bullying 112

© YouthLight, Inc.

Dedication

For my family – Mom, Dad, Mary, Christina, and Tab, with love.
To the memory of my grandmothers for giving me strength, hope, and courage
And a special thanks to Dr. Tamara Davis for everything, words cannot express my gratitude.

About the Author

Julia V. Taylor, Ph.D., is author of *The Body Image Workbook for Teens* and *Perfectly You*, and is coauthor of *G.I.R.L.S. (Girls in Real Life Situations)* and *The Bullying Workbook for Teens*. Taylor has worked as a middle and high school counselor and has a passion for empowering girls to stand up to unrealistic media expectations, take healthy risks, and cultivate meaningful relationships. Visit her online at www.juliavtaylor.com.

How to use this book

The purpose of *Salvaging Sisterhood* is to teach girls to communicate efficiently and effectively with one another. Often, adolescent girls will talk ***about*** who they are mad at, opposed to ***who*** they are mad at. *Salvaging Sisterhood* is designed to raise awareness, develop empathy, teach healthy conflict, explore feelings, and promote a positive change in female relationships. I have spent hours talking to adolescent girls about relational aggression. Of course, there are times when random groups of girls pick on an outsider for various reasons. However, the conflict, tension, and tears girls endure daily are generally invoked by their closest friends. Girls say that their closest friends are also their worst enemies because they truly "know" them, in turn, they know how to hurt them.

Salvaging Sisterhood can be used by professional school counselors, teachers, administrators, social workers, psychologists, and/or other professionals working with adolescent girls dealing with relational aggression. I have found girls to be reluctant to self-report relational aggression. Often times they believe the torture they deal with is normal and even a "rite of passage." Relying on teacher complaints, administrative complaints, the school nurse, and/or parent calls or concerns may be beneficial in identifying relational aggression.

The *Salvaging Sisterhood* book provides a pre/post test, group evaluations, a parental consent form, lesson plans and activities, affirmations, a certificate, suggestions for follow up activities, and an abundance of additional resources about relational aggression. The *Salvaging Sisterhood* curriculum is designed for a small group setting and should consist of one or two groups of friends (four to ten students). It is important that the girls generally get along. The goal of the group is to develop healthier relationships, not force them. Bully/victim situations should be dealt with on an individual basis. The *Salvaging Sisterhood* group should consist of eight forty-five minute sessions. Each session is designed around a theme and has many activity options to choose from based on the needs of your individual group. Each activity has journal topics to help the girls process the group outside of the

How to use this book
continued

school setting. In addition, this curriculum provides 80 affirmations for the girls to choose from during each group to help build and maintain individual self-esteem.

Upon completion of the group, a notification letter should be sent home to each girl's parent/guardian informing them that *Salvaging Sisterhood* has ended. In the letter, the parents should be informed that you will be checking in on the members both individually and as a group to review their progress.

Approximately four to six weeks after the group has ended, the group should be given a "follow up questionnaire" report to complete. This is a post-evaluation for the school counselor to review how the students are different as a result of the group. After the evaluations are turned in, the group should informally meet again to verbally express issues related to the group.

Other *Salvaging Sisterhood* Options
Although the intention for *Salvaging Sisterhood* is to be conducted in a small group format, most of the activities can be adapted for classroom counseling and large group settings.

Group Options

Often times, school counselors find it difficult to run groups in secondary schools. As part of ASCA's National Model, a comprehensive delivery system is essential to a successful school counseling program. The following are suggested times to run the *Salvaging Sisterhood* group.

Lunch Bunch
Allow the girls to leave class approximately five minutes early to get their lunch. Generally, each lunch session is about 30 minutes with an additional 10-15 minutes of bell time, allowing just enough time to squeeze group in.

Scattered Schedule
The group would meet during different classes each week, leaving little class time missed. For example:
Week One – First Period
Week Two – Second Period
Week Three – Third Period
Week Four – Forth Period
Week Five – Fifth Period
Week Six – Sixth Period
Week Seven – Seventh Period
Week Eight – Eighth Period

Group Options
continued

After School
If your school system runs activity buses and you are willing to stay a few extra minutes once a week, this time may work best. Running a group after school will be a lot less stressful to teachers and students concerned with missing class time.

Teacher Advisory Periods (TAP)
A lot of middle and high schools have their schedule adjusted to meet with the students for academic advising daily. This is a good time to gather a group if it does not involve different lunch shifts.

Group Activity Schedules
If your school holds Group Activities each week (extended homeroom) – this could be a perfect time to run a group.

Relational Aggression

The term "relational aggression" was developed in the early nineties by University of Minnesota researcher Dr. Nicki Crick. Crick found that girl's bullying behaviors generally focus on damaging an individual's social connections *within* the peer group (Crick & Grotpeter, 1995). Relational aggression refers to any act that actively excludes a person from making or maintaining friendships or being integrated into the peer group (Bjoerkqvist, Lagerspetz, & Kaukianen, 1992). Examples of relational aggression include, but are not limited to, spreading rumors, exclusion, social isolation, gossiping, eye-rolling, purposefully pitting friends against one another, using sarcasm at another's expense, reveling secrets of friends, and/or embellishing rumors.

The *Ophelia Project (n.d.)* is one of the first organizations to solely focus their work on creating a safe social climate for girls. Nicole Werner, *Ophelia Project* trainer, reported the following statistics about relational aggression:

- Children as young as preschool age use relational aggression, usually as a means to an end (e.g., getting a desired toy from a peer), rather than as retaliation.

- Relational aggression is not linked with socioeconomic status, meaning that children from all social classes use relational aggression.

- Boys are also relationally aggressive, although relational aggression is more common in girls' social circles than in boys. Relationally aggressive boys may, in fact, be "worse off" than girls in terms of their social adjustment, so it's important not to label relational aggression as "girl aggression!"

- Children who are highly relationally aggressive feel lonely and depressed, and they are likely to be disruptive in the classroom and to get into trouble frequently (according to teachers). They are also highly disliked by many of their classmates, although they do have friends. These results suggest that, even though relational aggressors appear to be the social "leaders," they feel badly about themselves and their social situations. We think these children are "at-risk" for serious future problems, such as delinquency and early substance use.

- Children who are the frequent victims of relational aggression are rejected, depressed, and submissive, and they have a poor self-concept in the areas of social relationships and physical attractiveness (Ophelia Project).

Behavior linked with relational aggression is often subtle and insidious, making it difficult to identify the perpetrator(s). If there is no blood, bruising, or classroom disruption, then where is the evidence? Bullying, sexual harass-

Relational Aggression
continued

ment, and other activities that students use to assert power and maintain their place in the pecking order are simultaneously pervasive and invisible, and as such, frequently overlooked by teachers and administrators (Perlstein, 2000). Educators and parents may not notice relational aggression because the behavior is often seen as "typical" (Casey-Cannon, Hayward, & Cowen, 2001).

Underwood (2003) suggests that teaching assertiveness to girls may reduce relational aggression. "Girls could be taught to express their needs and goals more directly, and helped to accept conflict may be a natural and even healthy part of close relationships" (Underwood, 2003). Casey-Cannon, et al. (2001) reported that a typical response to negative feelings associated with relational aggression (sadness, hurt, and/or anger) in adolescent girls was retaliation. The girls studied thought retaliation would change the aggressor. Underwood noted that teaching girls to intervene with each other, defending victims of relational aggression, may help reduce the negative effects of aggression.

Crick (2002) found that 70% of girls had been maltreated by their friends, causing significant adjustment difficulties. Relational aggression can lead to anxiety, substance abuse, school refusal, gang involvement, family problems, depression, eating disorders, and poor self-esteem. Adult women who were frequent victims are more likely to lean towards abusive relationships, have more unwanted pregnancies, and have a drug and/or alcohol addiction (Crick, 2002).

The issues around relational aggression directly effect peer relationships. Casey-Cannon, et al. (2001) indicated that frequent peer victimization was directly correlated with social isolation with girls who were insulted about characteristics they could not change (e.g., ethnicity). In addition, issues surrounding relational aggression negatively affect daily academic performance.

If students are being victimized at school, they are probably not thinking about an upcoming science test, homework, or their future. Empowering students to stand up for themselves and one another and to openly express feelings in a positive manner not only strengthens character, but can greatly improve the student's academic experience. Ultimately, I believe the law of inertia can conceptualize this issue – for every action – there is an equal and opposite reaction, meaning adolescents will react to overt actions taken against them. Taking time to raise awareness will eventually provoke change (Taylor, 2004).

© YouthLight, Inc.

ASCA National Standards

The American School Counselor Association (ASCA) National Standards

The ASCA National Standards for School Counseling Programs (Campbell & Dahir, 1997) provide a framework for developing and writing a school counseling program, as well as a description of the components of a quality school counseling program. More specifically, the purpose of the standards is to provide a model or guide to assist states, districts, and individual schools in planning, developing, implementing and evaluating a school counseling program which is comprehensive, developmental, and systematic. The National Standards focus on what all students, from pre-kindergarten through grade twelve, should know, understand, and be able to do to enhance their academic, career and personal/social development.

The National Standards for School Counseling Programs (Campbell & Dahir, 1997) facilitate student development in three areas: academic development, career development and personal/social development.

Salvaging Sisterhood falls within personal/social domain of the National Standards. Program standards for personal/ social development serve as a guide for the school counseling program to provide the foundation for personal and social growth which contributes to academic and career success. Listed on the next page are the standards and competencies the *Salvaging Sisterhood* curriculum aligns with.

ASCA National Standards

Standard A: Students will acquire the knowledge, attitudes and interpersonal skills to help them understand and respect self and others.

PS:A1 Acquire Self-knowledge

- PS:A1.1   Develop positive attitudes toward self as a unique and worthy person
- PS:A1.2   Identify values, attitudes and beliefs
- PS:A1.4   Understand change is a part of growth
- PS:A1.5   Identify and express feelings
- PS:A1.6   Distinguish between appropriate and inappropriate behavior
- PS:A1.7   Recognize personal boundaries, rights and privacy needs
- PS:A1.8   Understand the need for self-control and how to practice it
- PS:A1.9   Demonstrate cooperative behavior in groups
- PS:A1.10   Identify personal strengths and assets
- PS:A1.11   Identify and discuss changing personal and social roles
- PS:A1.12   Identify and recognize changing family roles

PS:A2 Acquire Interpersonal Skills

- PS:A2.1   Recognize that everyone has rights and responsibilities
- PS:A2.2   Respect alternative points of view
- PS:A2.3   Recognize, accept, respect and appreciate individual differences
- PS:A2.4   Recognize, accept and appreciate ethnic and cultural diversity
- PS:A2.5   Recognize and respect differences in various family configurations
- PS:A2.6   Use effective communications skills
- PS:A2.7   Know that communication involves speaking, listening and nonverbal behavior
- PS:A2.8   Learn how to make and keep friends

© YouthLight, Inc.

ASCA National Standards
continued

Standard B: Students will make decisions, set goals and take necessary action to achieve goals.

PS:B1 Self-knowledge Application

- PS:B1.1   Use a decision-making and problem-solving model
- PS:B1.2   Understand consequences of decisions and choices
- PS:B1.3   Identify alternative solutions to a problem
- PS:B1.4   Develop effective coping skills for dealing with problems
- PS:B1.5   Demonstrate when, where and how to seek help for solving problems and making decisions
- PS:B1.6   Know how to apply conflict resolution skills
- PS:B1.7   Demonstrate a respect and appreciation for individual and cultural differences
- PS:B1.8   Know when peer pressure is influencing a decision
- PS:B1.11   Use persistence and perseverance in acquiring knowledge and skills

Standard C: Students will understand safety and survival skills.

PS:C1 Acquire Personal Safety Skills

- PS:C1.4   Demonstrate the ability to set boundaries, rights and personal privacy
- PS:C1.7   Apply effective problem-solving and decision-making skills to make safe and healthy choices
- PS:C1.10   Learn techniques for managing stress and conflict
- PS:C1.11   Learn coping skills for managing life events

Source: Campbell, C.A., & Dahir, C.A. (1997). *Sharing the vision: The national standards for school counseling programs.* Alexandria, VA: American School Counselor Association.

Parent/Guardian Consent Form

To the parent/guardian of _____:

This letter is to inform you that I will soon be starting a group that I would like for your daughter to participate in. The group is titled *Salvaging Sisterhood* and is designed to raise awareness, develop empathy, teach healthy conflict, explore feelings, and promote a positive change in female relationships. *Salvaging Sisterhood* will meet for forty-five minutes, once a week, for eight weeks.

I sincerely hope that you will allow your daughter to participate, for I believe that she will truly benefit from Salvaging Sisterhood! Please detach and sign the permission slip below and have your daughter return it by_____. If you have any questions, please feel free to contact me.

Sincerely,

Professional School Counselor

Salvaging Sisterhood Consent Form

I give my daughter, _____ permission to participate in *Salvaging Sisterhood*. I understand that *Salvaging Sisterhood* will meet once a week for forty-five minutes, and that my daughter may miss a small portion of class while *Salvaging Sisterhood* is in session.

Parent/Guardian Signature_____

Contact Information (W)_____

(H) _____

© YouthLight, Inc.

Journaling

Journaling is a fun way to share secrets, goals, and good & bad times with yourself and friends. During Salvaging Sisterhood, you will keep a journal with you and bring it to every meeting – don't forget! You will have some topics to follow each week if you can't think of anything to write about. Everyone will have the opportunity to share what they wrote during each session, but you can always pass if you don't feel comfortable sharing. The last topic of each week is called "FESS UP!" When you are "fessing up" you are writing about something you may have done in the past related to the topic we discussed in group. For example, when we talk about gossip, you would "FESS UP" to a time you gossiped. If you are feeling super savvy, you can write about how you see the situation differently since discussing it in group. Don't think about what you are writing; just let your pen (or pencil) flow with the thoughts in your head and most importantly, HAVE FUN!

Declarations to Myself

LESSON 1: SALVAGING SISTERHOOD

Directions: The following statements are daily affirmations that can be used in many different ways to promote individual self-esteem among the girls. The declarations should be copied onto cardstock paper or index cards and placed in a container for the girls to randomly pick from each week. The girls should be encouraged to read them daily. They can be kept in their journals, be taped on their bathroom or bedroom mirrors, carried in their backpacks, or taped in their lockers.

I can dream about whatever I want!	I am achieving my goals!
I will live my life how I choose everyday!	I trust myself!
I respect myself!	I love myself!
I know my abilities!	I will choose to be happy today!
I use my strengths to be the best person I can be!	I am independent!
My friends will be there for me whenever I need them!	I can achieve anything I set my mind to!
I am smart!	I have high standards for myself!
I believe in myself!	I can do anything I put my mind to!

© YouthLight, Inc.

Declarations to Myself
continued

I have everything that I need!	I am an awesome role model to other girls!
I always have a choice!	I am going to be a successful adult!
I refuse to give into peer pressure!	I love myself!
I will never let anyone break my spirit!	I am an honest person!
I am worth any and everything!	I have a lot of self-worth!
I aim high to reach my goals!	I am a bold, courageous girl!
I know how to ask my friends for help if I need it!	I know that I am a miracle!
I totally believe in myself!	I am strong willed!
I am capable of making my dreams come true!	I am unique!
I follow my heart!	I am a super important person!
I listen to my body!	I live my life to the fullest everyday!

© YouthLight, Inc.

Declarations to Myself
continued

I trust my friends!	I am a kind person!
I make wise decisions!	I have a fabulous smile and spread sunshine everywhere I go!
I am full of energy and use it positively everyday!	I love my friends and family!
I accept people for who they are, not what they look like!	I am there for my friends when they need me!
I am a generous person!	I don't spread rumors about anyone!
I am special!	People can trust me all the time!
I have a fabulous sense of humor!	I am kind to people I don't know!
People want to be around me!	I stand by what I believe is right!
I share my stuff with my friends!	I don't judge anyone!
I am cheerful!	I don't care what other people think about me!
I have a great personality!	I accept myself all the time!

© YouthLight, Inc.

Declarations to Myself
continued

I have a great group of friends who love me no matter what!	I try to see the good side of everyone!
I have a great sense of humor!	I don't let my friends dictate what I do!
I learn from my mistakes!	I allow myself to make mistakes!
I allow my friends to make mistakes!	I am compassionate!
I am never mean spirited!	I am beautiful!
I am nice to myself!	I am realistic!
I am fun to hang out with!	I am the best woman I can be!
I listen to my instincts!	I control my thoughts!

© YouthLight, Inc.

Salvaging Sisterhood

LESSON 1: SALVAGING SISTERHOOD

Time: 45 minutes

Objectives:

❀ Girls will understand why they are participating in the group.
❀ Girls will understand confidentiality and group rules.
❀ Girls will be given journals to decorate and will understand how to use them each week.
❀ Girls will understand what relational agression is and why it is emotionally damaging.
❀ Girls will learn about positive self-talk.

Materials:

❀ Copy of *Salvaging Sisterhood* Pre-Group Survey for each girl
❀ Copy of "*Salvaging Sisterhood* Rules"
❀ A Journal or Notebook for each girl
❀ Pens, markers, glitter sticks, etc. for journal decorating
❀ Copy of "Journal Topics" for each girl
❀ "Declaration to Myself" cards

Activity: 40 minutes

❀ Explain to the girls why they have been chosen to participate in the group.
❀ Explain to the girls that the group is to help build their communication style with one another and strengthen their friendship.
❀ Hand out "*Salvaging Sisterhood* Rules" and go over them.
❀ Ask group members if they want to add anything.
❀ Have each group member autograph the group rules and remind them of importance of following the rules.
❀ Explain confidentiality and the consequences for breaking confidentiality.
❀ Hand out journals and allow girls to decorate them.
❀ While the girls are decorating their journals, ask and discuss the following questions:
  ✽ What is relational agression? (If they don't know, explain it to them.)
  ✽ How are girls mean to each other?
  ✽ Why are girls mean to each other?
  ✽ What happens when girls are mean to each other?

© YouthLight, Inc.

Salvaging Sisterhood
continued

LESSON 1: SALVAGING SISTERHOOD

- Is girl bullying different from guy bullying?
- Are girls suppose to be nice to each other?
- What do girls do when they get angry?
- Should girls get angry?
- What do your friends need to work on to make your friendship stronger?

❋ Talk to the girls about affirmations. Explain to the girls that each week they will be picking a "Declaration to Myself" to keep. Suggest to the girls that they tape their declarations to their bathroom or bedroom mirror, in their locker, in their journal, or keep them in their backpacks. Encourage the girls to repeat their declarations to themselves to remind them of how special and important they are.

Discussion: 5 minutes

❋ Ask the girls the following questions:
  - Did you feel comfortable during group?
  - Does anyone have any questions about the group, rules, or confidentiality?
  - How do you think you will benefit from the group?

Evaluation:

❋ Observe the overall reaction of the girls – did they seem comfortable? Withdrawn? Excited? Nervous? Open?
❋ Observe the body language and how the girls interacted with one another, especially during the journal decorating.
❋ Observe the girls willingness to use the weekly journals.

Homework:

❋ Journal Writing
  - In Salvaging Sisterhood today we...
  - What are some goals you have in *Salvaging Sisterhood*?
  - What kinds of girl bullying do you see with your friends?
  - FESS UP!

Salvaging Sisterhood

LESSON 1: SALVAGING SISTERHOOD

Pre-Group Survey

Directions: Please take a few moments to answer (HONESTLY) these questions. Only check one answer unless otherwise indicated.

1. Do you know a lot of "little details" about your friends? For example, their birthday, favorite color, how many brothers/sisters they have, their favorite food, etc.?

    ❑ Of course I do!   ❑ A few things.   ❑ Um, no!

2. Do your friends know a lot about you?

    ❑ Of course they do.   ❑ A few things.   ❑ No way!

3. Do you ever say things to your friends that are kind of mean, but then say "just kidding" or "SIKE" – but you really mean it?

    ❑ Yes.   ❑ No.   ❑ Sometimes.

4. If you hear some juicy news (true or not) about a friend do you:

    ❑ Keep it to yourself and not tell a soul, no matter what.
    ❑ Just tell your best friend and make her PROMISE not to tell anyone.
    ❑ Tell just the people you think should know.
    ❑ Tell everyone.

5. Would you stay home from a sleepover, party, movies, etc. if your friend was having a bad day and needed to talk to you?

    ❑ Always.
    ❑ It depends.
    ❑ No way, her problem will be there when I am available.

6. If you are having a problem with a friend, check two ways you would deal with it.

    ❑ Tell her.   ❑ Email her.
    ❑ Tell a friend.   ❑ Ask everyone if she is mad at me.
    ❑ Ignore it and hope it will go away.   ❑ Make up a rumor about her.
    ❑ Text her.   ❑ Don't invite her to a social gathering.

© YouthLight, Inc.

Salvaging Sisterhood

LESSON 1: SALVAGING SISTERHOOD

Group Rules

- Listen carefully and treat each girl with respect.
- What is said in the room – STAYS IN THE ROOM.
- Allow everybody to speak without interruption.
- Speak for yourself – not your "friends."
- If you are hurt or offended by what someone says, tell them, but tell them why it bothers you.
- Don't use specific names of people who are not present.
- Other rules:

_____

_____

_____

_____

Salvaging Sisterhood AUTOGRAPHS:

The Ties that Bind Us

LESSON 2: GIRL WORLD

Time: 45 minutes

Objectives:

- Girls will self-disclose.
- Girls will understand similarities between them.
- Girls will practice empathy.
- Girls will reflect and discuss important aspects of their lives.

Materials:

- "The Ties that Bind Us" questions, cut up, and placed in a container (basket, bowl, etc.)
- "Declaration to Myself" cards on pages 17-20

Opening: 5 minutes

- Journal discussion from previous week

Activity: 35 minutes

- Have the girls sit comfortably in a circle.
- Explain that the questions are to help the girls practice listening skills, empathy, and to self-disclose.
- Tell the girls they have the right to pass.
- Select a girl to pick a question, read it outloud, and answer it in a timely fashion.
- Depending on the *Salvaging Sisterhood* dynamics, discussion may be used.
- Repeat this process until the time is up.
- Have each girl pick a "Declaration to Myself" card.
- Thank the girls for sharing.

The Ties that Bind Us
continued

LESSON 2: GIRL WORLD

Discussion: 5 minutes

- Ask the girls the following questions:
  - How did you feel being put on the spot?
  - How did you feel answering the questions?
  - What did you think the other girls were thinking?
  - How did you feel listening to other girl's questions?

Evaluation:

- Observe and confront any silent girls privately.
- Observe the body language of the girls while answering questions.
- Observe the attention level of the girls while others are talking.

Homework:

- Journal Writing
  - In Salvaging Sisterhood today we...
  - What is cool about being a girl?
  - What makes being a girl hard?
  - FESS UP!

The Ties that Bind Us Questions

LESSON 2: GIRL WORLD

What would your social life be like if you didn't have school?	How do you feel when you hear a juicy piece of gossip about someone else?
If you could go shopping with anyone in the world, who would you go with?	How do you feel when you hear gossip about yourself that is totally not true?
What was the most embarrassing thing that ever happened to you?	If you could change one thing about yourself, would you?
What is your biggest fear?	Do you dress in clothes you like or clothes your friends like?
Do you think reality shows are reality?	What is something that is not so perfect about your family?
What is the best reality TV show? Why?	If you had one wish, anything, what would it be?

© YouthLight, Inc.

The Ties that Bind Us Questions
continued

What is one thing that nobody really knows about you?	Talk about one time that you felt totally fake.
Is it hard for you to admit when you are wrong? Why or why not?	Is there something you like to do, but don't because you are afraid that someone will think it is not "cool?"
When someone says something mean to you, then says "Just kidding" – do you think they are? How do you feel?	What is the most misunderstood thing about you?
Do you fight fair, or talk behind people's backs? Give an example of each.	How would your best friend describe your personality?
What is the meanest thing you have ever done to a friend?	What is the best thing about you?
What is your favorite thing about yourself?	Have you ever made anyone cry?
Do guys have it easier than girls?	Who is the coolest person at your school? Why are they so cool?

© YouthLight, Inc.

The Ties that Bind Us Questions *continued*

What is one thing that your parent/s or guardian just DON'T understand?	What would the world be like without gossip?
Do boys have it easy?	Have you ever spread an untrue rumor? If yes, why?
What is the best thing about being a girl?	No social media or no phone for a year, which would you choose?
What is the worst thing about being a girl?	What is the best thing about your friends?
What is peer pressure?	Do girls bully more than boys?
What is gossip?	Do girls forgive more than boys?
Is all gossip bad?	What is the number one thing that girls fight about?

© YouthLight, Inc.

Sisterhood Rocks!

LESSON 2: GIRL WORLD

Time: 45 minutes

Objectives:

- Girls will explore their feelings about being a girl.
- Girls will understand that they have similar issues with girlhood.

Opening: 5 minutes

- Journal discussion from previous week

Materials:

- "T.G.I.F." Worksheet
- "Declaration to Myself" cards

Activity: 35 minutes

- Ask the girls, "What does it mean to be a girl?" Generate a discussion and encourage creative thinking.
- Ask the girls, "What is hard about being a girl" and/or "Do boys have it easier than girls?"
- Hand out the worksheet "T.G.I.F."
- Read the directions out loud and see how many additional reasons the girls can come up with.
- Explore their comments and discuss their reactions to each other's statements.
- Have each girl pick a "Declaration to Myself" card.
- Thank the girls for sharing.

Sisterhood Rocks!
continued

LESSON 2: GIRL WORLD

Discussion – 5 minutes

- Ask the group members the following questions:
  - How is being a girl empowering?
  - How can girls stick together?
  - How will you embrace your girlhood in the future?

Evaluation:

- Did the girls seem embarrassed during the discussions?
- Do the girls come up with any deep reasons they like about being a girl?

Homework:

- Journal Writing
  - In Salvaging Sisterhood today we…
  - What is cool about being a girl?
  - What makes being a girl difficult?
  - FESS UP!

© YouthLight, Inc.

T.G.I.F. – Thank Goodness I'm Female

LESSON 2: GIRL WORLD

There are so many great things about being a girl. Below are ten reasons being a girl is awesome. What does being a girl mean to you and your friends? Why is being a girl cool? See how many reasons you can come up with.

1. Girls can wear whatever clothes they want.
2. Girls are more emotional.
3. Girls can have babies.
4. Girls can wear makeup.
5. Girls can do their hair differently everyday.
6. Girls can wear cool smelling lotions.
7. Girls can play any sport they want.
8. Girls can paint their nails different colors.
9. Girls can curl their eyelashes.
10. Girls can cry in front of their friends and not get made fun of.
11. _____
12. _____
13. _____
14. _____
15. _____
16. _____
17. _____
18. _____
19. _____
20. _____

© YouthLight, Inc.

Sisterhood Style

LESSON 2: GIRL WORLD

Time: 45 minutes

Objectives:

- Girls will self-disclose.
- Girls will listen to others.
- Girls will reflect and discuss their personality traits.
- Girls will discuss their friendship strengths.

Materials:

- "Sisterhood Style Quiz" worksheet
- Art materials (markers, crayons, glitter, glue, pens, pencils)
- Poster board or large piece of paper
- "Declaration to Myself" cards

Opening: 5 minutes

- Journal discussion from previous week

Activity: 35 minutes

- Have the girls sit around the table.
- Ask the girls the following questions:
    - What makes you unique?
    - What makes other people unique?
    - Would the world be boring if everyone was the same?
    - Why is being different important?
- After the girls have discussed the questions, distribute the worksheet, "Sisterhood Style Quiz."
- Have the girls complete the worksheet and then discuss the results, making sure the girls recognize the importance of their strengths.
- Have the girls make a friendship poster using words that describe the unique characteristics that make up their friendship.
- Display the poster somewhere visible.
- Have each girl pick a "Declaration to Myself" card.
- Thank the girls for sharing.

© YouthLight, Inc.

LESSON 2: GIRL WORLD

Discussion: 5 minutes

- Ask the girls the following questions:
    - What did you learn today about your personality?
    - In what ways does your style enhance your friendships?

Evaluation:

- Observe and confront any silent girls privately.
- Observe the participation and sharing level while the girls are working together on the poster.
- Observe the amount of conflict, and the resolution style, if the girls do not agree with one another's self-observation.

Homework:

- Journal Writing
    - In Salvaging Sisterhood today we...
    - What is cool about being a girl?
    - What makes being a girl hard?
    - FESS UP!

Sisterhood Style Quiz

LESSON 2: GIRL WORLD

Everybody has a unique sisterhood style. Our unique styles are what bond us together and help build terrific friendships. Below you will find six different sisterhood personality types. Check all of the qualities you believe you have and when you are done, see where you checked the most. That is your very own, unique sisterhood personality type. Afterwards, share your results with your friends and see if they agree or disagree with you.

The Believer

- ❏ I am full of energy.
- ❏ I always have a purpose.
- ❏ I stand up for what I believe in.
- ❏ I don't slow down unless somebody tells me to.
- ❏ I always reflect on my actions.
- ❏ I trust people.

The Adventurer

- ❏ I am brave.
- ❏ I can pick up on how others are feeling.
- ❏ I am unique and don't follow the crowd.
- ❏ I learn from my mistakes.
- ❏ I can be defensive when I know I am right.
- ❏ I know how to push people's buttons to get what I want.

The Initiator

- ❏ I am generally happy and see the good in everyone.
- ❏ I am really smart.
- ❏ I think outside of the box.
- ❏ I am always planning our social activities.
- ❏ I am a dreamer.
- ❏ I am a leader.

© YouthLight, Inc.

Sisterhood Style Quiz

continued

LESSON 2: GIRL WORLD

The Energizer

- ❏ I am full of energy.
- ❏ I do things I love.
- ❏ I talk with my hands.
- ❏ I have lots of friends in different groups.
- ❏ I can get along with everyone.
- ❏ I love attention.

The Chatterbox

- ❏ I am always talking to someone.
- ❏ I hate to be alone.
- ❏ I can talk my friends into anything.
- ❏ I love to teach people things.
- ❏ I get told to be quiet a lot.
- ❏ I make friends easily.

The Competitor

- ❏ I inspire people to be better.
- ❏ I try to make people change their minds.
- ❏ I love to argue.
- ❏ I am a leader.
- ❏ I usually get what I want.
- ❏ I don't admit to mistakes too often.

© YouthLight, Inc.

Illustrating Us

LESSON 2: GIRL WORLD

Time: 45 minutes

Objectives:

❀ Girls will creatively create a mural that describes their friendship.
❀ Girls will work together and agree upon ideas/suggestions.

Materials:

❀ Magazines
❀ Newspaper
❀ Poster Board
❀ Scissors
❀ Glue/Tape
❀ "Declaration to Myself" cards

Opening: 5 minutes

❀ Journal discussion from previous week

Activity: 35 minutes

❀ Ask the girls to think about their friendship. Go around the circle and have each girl say an adjective that describes their friendship.
❀ Tell the girls they will be creating a poster that describes their friendship. Encourage them to be creative and find individual characteristics that make their friendship special.
❀ Hand out materials and have the girls work together to cut out words, phrases, quotes, and/or pictures they find meaningful.
❀ When the girls are finished, have them paste/tape their materials to the poster board.
❀ Ask the girls to name their poster.
❀ Display it somewhere visible.
❀ Have each girl pick a "Declaration to Myself" card.
❀ Thank the girls for sharing.

© YouthLight, Inc.

A Picture of Us
continued

LESSON 2: GIRL WORLD

Discussion: 5 Minutes

* Ask the girls the following questions:
  * Was it easy to get along?
  * Were anyone's ideas rejected?
  * Does everyone think the poster accurately describes their clique?

Evaluation:

* Observe the work ethic of the girls with each other.
* Observe whether or not each thought/idea was utilized.
* Observe any friction between the girls.

Homework:

* Journal Writing
  * In Salvaging Sisterhood today we...
  * What is cool about being a girl?
  * What makes being a girl difficult?
  * FESS UP!

Our Friendship

LESSON 3: FRIENDS

Time: 45 minutes

Objectives:

❀ Girls will become aware of the qualities they seek in a friend.
❀ Girls will learn about their friendship styles.
❀ Girls will learn what other people look for in a friend.

Materials:

❀ Copies of "True Friend..." worksheet for each girl
❀ Copies of "Am I a Good Friend?" for each girl
❀ "Declaration to Myself" cards

Opening: 5 minutes

❀ Journal discussion from previous week

Activity: 35 minutes

❀ Welcome the girls back and remind them of the rules and confidentiality.
❀ Hand out "A True Friend..." and have each girl complete the worksheet.
❀ Ask the girls to share and facilitate conversation by asking the following questions:
  ❦ Did any of your rankings surprise you?
  ❦ Have you ever thought about what you look for in a friend?
  ❦ Do your friends match your rankings?
  ❦ What do you think your rankings say about you as a friend?
  ❦ Do you think you would rank yourself the way you rank your friends?
  ❦ How do you feel about being "ranked?"
❀ Hand out "Am I a Good Friend?" and have each girl complete it.
❀ Allow the girls to self-score and discuss the questions.
❀ Have each girl pick a "Declaration to Myself" card.
❀ Thank the girls for sharing.

Our Friendship
continued

LESSON 3: FRIENDS

Discussion: 5 minutes

- Ask girls the following questions:
    - What did you learn about yourself?
    - What qualities do you value in a friendship?
    - Talk about some things you need to work on.

Evaluation:

- Observe the participation level of the girls.
- Observe the amount of self-disclosure within the girls.
- Observe whether their friends agree with what they say.

Homework:

- Journal Writing
    - In Salvaging Sisterhood today we...
    - What are some things you learned about yourself?
    - What are some things you learned about your friends?
    - FESS UP!

© YouthLight, Inc.

LESSON 3: FRIENDS

A True Friend...

What Do I Look for in a True Friend?

Sometimes it is important for us to reflect upon what we really look for in a friend. Some things you may already know, and some could totally shock you! Rank the friend qualities below in order from:
1 (ABSOLUTE MOST IMPORTANT QUALITY) to
15 ("DOSEN'T MATTER TO ME" QUALITY)

_____ How smart they are
_____ What kind of home they live in
_____ The brand of clothes they wear
_____ How honest they are
_____ What their hair looks like
_____ How much they listen to you when you have a problem
_____ If they like the same movies/TV shows as you
_____ What kind of car their parents drive
_____ How much fun you have with them
_____ How popular they are
_____ What religion they are
_____ How much you can trust them
_____ How much they gossip about other people
_____ What size they are
_____ How dependable they are

1. Read carefully over what you ranked and write down one thing you learned about yourself.

2. Is there anything else that is important to you in a friendship?

3. Write down some things that you would like to change about how you pick your friends.

© YouthLight, Inc.

Am I A Good Friend?

LESSON 3: FRIENDS

1. Do you feel like you cannot be totally honest with your friends?

    Never　　　　　Sometimes　　　　　Usually　　　　　Always

2. Do you get bored with your friends if you are not gossiping about someone else?

    Never　　　　　Sometimes　　　　　Usually　　　　　Always

3. Do you talk about your friends behind their back?
   Even if it is just something minor?

    Never　　　　　Sometimes　　　　　Usually　　　　　Always

4. Do you have trouble remembering your friends' birthdays and what religious beliefs they have?

    Never　　　　　Sometimes　　　　　Usually　　　　　Always

5. Do you ever purposefully leave your friends out of your group – like if you all go to the movies, to dinner, or in the cafeteria at lunch?

    Never　　　　　Sometimes　　　　　Usually　　　　　Always

Am I A Good Friend?
continued

LESSON 3: FRIENDS

6. Do you start your sentences off with, "Don't tell anyone I told you this... BUT?"

   Never   Sometimes   Usually   Always

7. Do you make all of the decisions about where to hang out or what to do on the weekends or after-school?

   Never   Sometimes   Usually   Always

8. If you have plans to go to the mall with your friends, then something better comes along, do you cancel?

   Never   Sometimes   Usually   Always

9. Do you lie to your friends? For example, your friend asks if you like her shoes and you really don't - do you tell her you do?

   Never   Sometimes   Usually   Always

10. Do you feel like your friendships are one-sided? For example, do you do all of the calling and texting or do you rely on someone else?

    Never   Sometimes   Usually   Always

© YouthLight, Inc.

Am I A Good Friend?

continued

LESSON 3: FRIENDS

11. Do you ever make fun of other people and hurt their feelings – even by accident?

    Never   Sometimes   Usually   Always

12. Do you wait for other people to apologize to you if you are in a fight?

    Never   Sometimes   Usually   Always

13. If a new girl moves to town, and your friend hangs out with her, do you get jealous?

    Never   Sometimes   Usually   Always

14. If your friend does not call you back when you called her and it was really important, do you get angry?

    Never   Sometimes   Usually   Always

15. Do you ever think your friends are annoying?

    Never   Sometimes   Usually   Always

© YouthLight, Inc.

LESSON 3: FRIENDS

16. If you go on vacation with your friends for two weeks would you be fighting after a few days?

   Never   Sometimes   Usually   Always

17. Do you ditch your friends when you like a guy?

   Never   Sometimes   Usually   Always

18. Have you ever gossiped online about your friend and denied it?

   Never   Sometimes   Usually   Always

19. If your friend was having trouble in math and had to stay after school for tutoring – but you two had plans to hang out, would you get mad?

   Never   Sometimes   Usually   Always

20. Do you ever think "why do I like her" about any of your friends?

   Never   Sometimes   Usually   Always

Am I A Good Friend?
continued

LESSON 3: FRIENDS

How did you do?

❦ Give yourself three points for every "Never"
❦ Give yourself two points for every "Sometimes"
❦ Give yourself one point for every "Usually"
❦ Give yourself one point for every "Always"

If you scored:

45-60:

You are an awesome friend! You trust your friends and can confide in them. You help them when they need it, and are so comfortable around them that you don't worry that they will stab you in the back! You ROCK!

20-44:

Your friendships are rocky. If you go back and look at the answers, perhaps you can work on ways to improve your friendships! Your answers may reveal ways that you can help your friendship by being more open and honest – let's talk about them!

Less than 20:

Sister – you are having major friend issues! You need to do some serious evaluation of yourself, your friends, and what you want out of these friendships! Look deep inside yourself – not on the surface of your friends!

© YouthLight, Inc.

It's All About Me

LESSON 3: FRIENDS

Time: 45 minutes

Objectives:

- Girls will self-disclose.
- Girls will examine how much they know about each other.
- Girls will practice listening skills.
- Girls will reflect and discuss important aspects of their lives.

Materials:

- Handout – "So, You Think you Know Me?"
- Each girl's name written down and folded, in a container
- Writing Utensil
- "Declaration to Myself" cards

Opening: 5 minutes

- Journal discussion from previous group

Activity: 35 minutes

- Have the girls sit around a table and hand out materials.
- Have the girls draw a name.
- Tell the girls to begin the worksheet (10 minutes).
- When the girls are done, have each one reveal who they picked.
- Have each girl share and compare their questions.
- Have each girl pick a "Declaration to Myself" card.
- Thank the girls for sharing.

© YouthLight, Inc.

It's All About Me

continued

LESSON 3: FRIENDS

Discussion: 5 minutes

❃ Ask the girls the following questions:
- ✽ Was this activity easy or hard? Why?
- ✽ How did you feel answering the questions?
- ✽ Were you worried about who had you and what they were writing? If so share why:
- ✽ How did you feel listening to other girls' questions?

Evaluation:

❃ Observe the body language of the girls while reading questions.
❃ Observe the attention level of the girls while others are sharing.

Homework:

❃ Journal Writing
- ✽ In Salvaging Sisterhood today we...
- ✽ What are some things you learned about yourself?
- ✽ What are some things you learned about your friends?
- ✽ FESS UP!

© YouthLight, Inc.

So, You Think You Know Me?

LESSON 3: FRIENDS

Do you think you know everything about your best friends? You might be surprised. On the first part, answer the questions about you. For the second part write the answers about the name you picked. After everyone is done, you will find out how much you really know. Good Luck!

All about _____
(your name)

My favorite color is _____
My favorite movie is _____
My favorite sport/hobby is _____
My bedroom is decorated with _____
My favorite subject is _____
My birthday is _____
My favorite food is _____
My favorite outfit is _____
My favorite song is _____
My best quality is _____

All about _____
(your friend's name)

Her favorite color is _____
Her favorite movie is _____
Her favorite sport/hobby is _____
Her bedroom is decorated with _____
Her favorite subject is _____
Her birthday is _____
Her favorite food is _____
Her favorite outfit is _____
Her favorite song is _____
Her best quality is _____

© YouthLight, Inc.

Examining Friendships

LESSON 3: FRIENDS

Time: 45 minutes

Objectives:

* Girls will examine the different roles they play within their friendship.
* Girls will learn the hierarchy of friendships.

Materials:

* Paper
* Writing utensil
* "Declaration to Myself" cards

Opening: 5 minutes

* Journal discussion from previous week

Activity: 35 minutes

* Start off discussing the different roles we play in different situations. For example, at school you are a student. At home you are a daughter and/or a sister. If you are a sister, you are an older, younger, or middle sibling. On the soccer team you are the goalie, etc. Ask the girls to discuss the different roles they play in life.
* Now ask the girls what role they play in their friendships. After a general discussion, ask the girls the following questions:
  * Who makes the decisions?
  * What are the rules within your group of friends?
  * Who makes up the rules?
  * Who consults with whom when there is a problem?
  * What happens if someone breaks a rule?
  * What do you do with your friends? (example – shop, have sleepovers, social media) and what do you do individually (play a sport, band)?
  * Are those differences important?
  * Does somebody decide where you sit at lunch?
  * Is someone in the group more important than another person?
  * Does someone in the group think they are more important than the others?
  * Do you all act the same way when your friends are not around?

Examining Friendships

LESSON 3: FRIENDS

- What are some things you do differently when you are with other friends and/or family?
- Could you switch roles if you wanted to?
- What if someone is mad at someone else – does somebody take over her role?
- What about if someone is absent from school – is she replaced for the day? If so, what is different?
* Ask the girls to write down three things that they like about their friends, and three things they wish were different.
* Collect the papers and read over them later to assess what work needs to be done in *Salvaging Sisterhood*.
* Have each girl pick a "Declaration to Myself" card.
* Thank the girls for sharing.

Discussion: 5 Minutes

* Ask the girls the following questions:
  - Was this lesson easy or difficult? Why?
  - How could your friendships grow closer?

Evaluation:

* Observe the amount of tension when discussing the questions.
* Observe the body language of the girls – was it open or did anyone seem shut down?
* Examine who did most of the talking and if there were specific "leaders" and "followers" in the group.

Homework:

* Journal Writing
  - In Salvaging Sisterhood today we...
  - What are some things you learned about yourself?
  - What are some things you learned about your friends?
  - FESS UP!

Oh No She Did Not!

LESSON 4: BEING MEAN

Time: 45 minutes

Objectives:

- Girls will learn how their words may affect others.
- Girls will demonstrate to each other how they have been negatively affected by comments.
- Girls will learn to think before they speak.

Materials:

- "Oh No She Did Not" worksheet for each girl
- "Declaration to Myself" cards

Opening: 5 minutes

- Journal discussion from previous week

Activity: 35 minutes

- Ask the girls what sarcasm means.
- Ask each girl how sarcasm has affected them.
- Hand out "Oh No She Did Not" and discuss each scenario and question after they role play.
    - How does each situation put another girl down?
    - How does the behavior cause conflict?
    - Can the situations be turned around?
    - Can anything constructive be said?
    - What could have been done differently?
    - Why do girls do this to each other?
- Have each girl pick a "Declaration to Myself" card.
- Thank the girls for sharing.

© YouthLight, Inc.

Oh No She Did Not!
continued

LESSON 4: BEING MEAN

Discussion: 5 minutes

- ❊ Ask the girls the following questions:
    - ✤ What did you learn in *Salvaging Sisterhood* today?
    - ✤ How can you avoid using sarcasm negatively?
    - ✤ Are you more comfortable giving a compliment?

Evaluation:

- ❊ Observe the participation level of the girls.
- ❊ Observe the amount of self-disclosure used in discussion.
- ❊ Observe attention levels of the girls while completing role plays.
- ❊ Do they seem to "get it" or are they blowing it off?

Homework:

- ❊ Journal Writing
    - ✤ In Salvaging Sisterhood today we...
    - ✤ Write about a time a friend was mean to you.
    - ✤ How do you feel about *Salvaging Sisterhood* so far?
    - ✤ FESS UP!

Oh No She Did Not! Worksheet

LESSON 4: BEING MEAN

Some comments we make can put people down – even if we don't mean what we say. Sometimes people are not aware of how sarcasm hurts other people's feelings. Often people will say "just kidding" or "I didn't REALLY mean it" or "stop being so sensitive!" Below are some typical scenarios that could cause major friend problems. Role play each scenario and then discuss it with the group.

Role Play #1
You are wearing a new outfit to school. Your best friend tells your other friend that your new outfit is ugly. When you confront her, she says "I was just kidding, can't you take a joke?" What is your reaction? How do you handle it?

Role Play #2
Your friend tells everyone that you made out with the boy you like after school and you didn't. She claims that she heard you did and says, "What's the big deal? I thought I was helping your popularity." How would you react?

Role Play #3
You like a boy in class that is not very popular. When you confess to your friend she exclaims, "He is such a dork. I so cannot talk to you if you two are going out!" When you get upset, she says, "I wasn't being serious. Get a grip!" Would you still like him? Would you be upset with your friend?

Role Play #4
You have nothing to do on a Saturday night and overhear two friends talking about going to the mall and having a sleepover. When you ask if you can come, one girl says, "Sure, only if you promise not to talk. SIKE." They are mean to you for the rest of the day. Would you still go? Would you ask another friend to talk to her and see what is going on? Explain.

Role Play #5
Your friends are ignoring you and you don't know what you did. When you confront them and ask what is wrong they say, "Nothing." You KNOW something is up. You have been getting the silent treatment for days now and it is making you CRAZY! What would you do?

Role Play #6
You want to go out with a friend to see a movie but don't want your other friend to come because you spend too much time with her. When she finds out she starts spreading rumors about you. How do you react? What do you do?

© YouthLight, Inc.

Sticks and Stones

LESSON 4: BEING MEAN

Time: 45 minutes

Objectives:

- Girls will self-disclose.
- Girls will learn how to give a compliment.
- Girls will learn the difference between constructive and destructive criticism.

Materials:

- "The Chain of Compliments" worksheet for each girl
- "Constructive vs. Destructive Criticism" worksheet for each girl
- Writing Utensil
- "Declaration to Myself" cards

Opening: 5 minutes

- Journal discussion

Activity: 35 minutes

- Hand out "The Chain of Compliments" worksheet to each girl.
- Ask the girls how they give a compliment.
- Ask the girls how they take a compliment.
- Read over worksheet and initiate discussion with the girls.
- Ask the girls what the difference between constructive and destructive criticism is.
- Hand out "Constructive vs. Destructive Criticism" worksheet.
- Read each scenario out loud and have the girls generate and agree upon a response.
- Have each girl pick a "Declaration to Myself" card.
- Thank the girls for sharing.

© YouthLight, Inc.

Sticks and Stones

continued

LESSON 4: BEING MEAN

Discussion: 5 minutes

- Ask the girls the following questions:
    - What did you learn during this activity?
    - How do you give and receive compliments?
    - In the future, how will you handle destructive criticism?

Evaluation:

- Observe the girls reaction when learning about compliment styles – do they seem to understand how to take a compliment?
- Observe the seriousness of the girls while discussing criticism.

Homework:

- Journal Writing
    - In Salvaging Sisterhood today we...
    - Write about a time a friend was mean to you.
    - How do you feel about *Salvaging Sisterhood* so far?
    - FESS UP!

The Chain of Compliments

LESSON 4: BEING MEAN

How do you start off conversations with your friends? Are you always looking for negatives? Do you give compliments often? Do you expect them back? Some people indirectly ask for compliments – for example they may say, "My hair looks terrible today," – just so someone will say, "No, it looks fine." What is your comliment style? Below are a few suggestions for giving, and taking, a compliment.

Three things that are easy to address are:

Peoples' outfit – "You look totally cute today," "I love that shirt," or "Are those new shoes? They look great on you!"

Their features – "Your eye shadow is so cool." "I like your nail polish!"

Something great that they did – "I heard you got an A on that Science test – awesome!" Or, "Great soccer game last night!"

Responding to a compliment:

Responding to a compliment is a little bit trickier. Sometimes you may think you have to say something "nice" about the person that complimented you. Other times you may feel like you have to ignore the compliment and say the exact opposite! For example, let's say your friend says, "Your hair looks great today." Instead of saying, "So does yours," or "OMG, it looks terrible," you could simply reply, "Thanks, that made me feel really good."

Remember – compliments acknowledge, are thoughtful, and specific. Try giving (and taking) one today.

© YouthLight, Inc.

Constructive vs. Destructive Criticism

LESSON 4: BEING MEAN

 Your friend is wearing a new outfit and you don't think it looks good on her. She asks you, "Do you like this on me?" How would you respond? Would you tell her you love it and lie? Would you tell her you don't care for it? Being honest is difficult sometimes. Below you will find a list of criticisms. Circle either "constructive" or "destructive" under each question. Try to see if you can come up with a constructive sentence for the destructive ones. Good Luck!

Those shoes are so last year!

        Constructive   Destructive

You have a ton of zits. Do you want to borrow my makeup?

        Constructive   Destructive

I think you could do a lot better, but if you want to go out with him that's cool!

        Constructive   Destructive

That perfume isn't my favorite, but I'm not wearing it!

        Constructive   Destructive

I wish you wouldn't call me so late; my parents go to bed early and wake up yelling at me!

        Constructive   Destructive

That skirt is so totally short, how are you going to sit down?

        Constructive   Destructive

That haircut isn't the greatest, but it will grow out!

        Constructive   Destructive

When was the last time you looked in the mirror?

        Constructive   Destructive

© YouthLight, Inc.

Sugar & Spice, and Everything Nice...

LESSON 4: BEING MEAN

Time: 45 minutes

Objectives:

❧ Girls will learn the difference between being mean and venting.
❧ Girls will demonstrate coping mechanisms using role-playing.
❧ Girls will learn who they should and should not vent to.

Materials:

❧ "If You Don't Have Anything Nice to Say, Don't Let Anyone Hear You Say It!" worksheet for each girl
❧ "Declaration to Myself" cards

Opening: 5 minutes

❧ Journal discussion from previous week

Activity: 35 minutes

❧ Ask the girls about the last time someone really annoyed them.
❧ Ask the girls what the difference between being mean and venting is.
❧ Explain to them, if needed, that we all need to vent sometimes to help us cope with the differences among us, but it is all about our intentions for venting – why are we doing it?
❧ Hand out "If You Don't Have Anything Nice to Say, Don't Let Anyone Hear You Say It!" and follow the directions on the activity sheet.
❧ Have each girl pick a "Declaration to Myself" card.
❧ Thank the girls for sharing.

Sugar & Spice, and Everything Nice...
continued

LESSON 4: BEING MEAN

Discussion: 5 minutes

- Ask the girls the following questions:
    - What is the difference between being mean and venting?
    - When someone is annoying you, how can you cope?
    - Who can you trust?

Evaluation:

- Observe the seriousness of the girls when doing the role-plays.
- Observe the amount of self-disclosure used in discussion.
- Observe "blaming" behaviors with the girls.

Homework:

- Journal Writing
    - In Salvaging Sisterhood today we...
    - Write about a time a friend was mean to you.
    - How do you feel about *Salvaging Sisterhood* so far?
    - FESS UP!

© YouthLight, Inc.

If You Don't Have Anything Nice To Say...

LESSON 4: BEING MEAN

Do you believe that title? We all have said something about a friend that we later regret. It is perfectly normal to get angry and vent, it is actually very healthy! However, it is all about how you vent and your intentions (reasons) for venting. Think for a minute about the last time you were mad at a friend and told someone else.

1. Why were you mad? _____

2. Who did you tell? (Check all that apply)
   ❏ My family   ❏ My School Counselor   ❏ A Teacher
   ❏ 1 friend   ❏ 2 friends   ❏ 3 or more friends   ❏ Someone else

3. Why did you tell them? (Check all that apply)
   ❏ Because I was SO mad!
   ❏ Because I wanted them to be mad at her too!
   ❏ Because I needed help coping with it!
   ❏ Because I needed to know that I AM right!
   ❏ Because I was really upset and needed someone to just listen to me!
   ❏ I don't know, I just did!

4. How did you feel after you talked about it? (Check all that apply)
   ❏ Great!
   ❏ A little bit better, but I was still a little angry.
   ❏ I am STILL mad!

5. Did talking about it help?   ❏ Yes   ❏ No

Sometimes you don't need to talk directly to a friend when they do something that irritates you. Sometimes you need to tell somebody else. It is better to tell someone you trust that you just need to vent – that way you don't look two-faced when you are still nice to the person you are a little annoyed at. Each of the situations on the following page has a theme – the annoying behavior or incident will probably stop. Is it worth a fight?

© YouthLight, Inc.

If You Don't Have Anything Nice To Say...
continued

LESSON 4: BEING MEAN

Be creative and role-play with the group and see what you think about each situation. After you have finished each role play, discuss the following questions:

1. What is bothersome about the situation?
2. Why is it bothersome?
3. Will the behavior stop sometime soon?
4. Who could you talk to about it?
5. Do you really need to talk about it? Could you journal instead? Could you go for a run or walk? Can you understand their point of view?

Role-Play #1
Amy has been so annoying lately. She won the "Most Valuable Soccer Player" award and has not stopped talking about if for like three days. I want to shove her award down her throat.

Role-Play #2
Shayna just started going out with Sean two days ago and all she ever wants to talk about is him. I get so sick of it. When I message or text her, she is talking to him. When I call her, she is on the phone with him. When she writes me notes in class, she writes "I LOVE Sean" all over the paper. She wants to bring him everywhere. I hope they break up soon.

Role-Play #3
Lisa can't hang out with us until she raises her English grade. Her Mom caught her on her cell phone at 11:00 pm and grounded her. I am so bummed because we were all supposed to have a sleepover at her house this weekend and now we can't. She ruined my weekend!

Role-Play #4
Sabrina cannot make her mind up about anything. She called me 10 times this morning to see what she should wear and when we finally made a decision, she came to school in the first outfit she called me about. She is just trying to impress Ben and he wears the same stupid jersey everyday. Like he cares what she is wearing!

Did You Hear About...

LESSON 5: GIRL TALK

Time: 45 minutes

Objectives:

- Girls will consider the role gossip plays in their conversations.
- Girls will consider how gossip affects their lives and the lives of others.
- Girls will become aware of how much they participate in gossip.

Opening: 5 minutes

- Journal discussion from previous week

Materials:

- A large bowl filled with water
- A rock or pebble
- "Declaration to Myself" cards

Activity: 35 minutes

- Have one girl drop the rock/pebble into the water. The rock will produce a ripple effect. Have a discussion as to how this relates to gossip with the girls.
- Ask the girls to define gossip.
- Ask the girls what life would be like without gossip.
- Ask the girls if gossip can be avoided.
- Ask the following questions and encourage discussion:
  - Is there a difference between positive and negative gossip?
  - How have you been hurt by gossip?
  - When you spread gossip and are later confronted, how do you react?
  - Do your friends think you are a gossip?
  - When you hear some juicy gossip about somebody – do you add more to the story before telling somebody else?
  - Do boys gossip?
  - How does gossip hurt others?
  - What if it is true? Can it still be hurtful?

© YouthLight, Inc.

Did You Hear About...
continued

LESSON 5: GIRL TALK

- * Can you be a gossip addict?
  * Can you be trusted with a secret?
  * What if a friend is in serious trouble – do you tell an adult or a friend?
  * If you could make up a policy about "bad" gossip – and the whole school had to follow it – what would it look like?
  * Is there a way for you to help others stop spreading rumors?
  * What are some ways that the school can help with gossiping?
- Have each girl pick a "Declaration to Myself!" Card.
- Thank the girls for sharing.

Discussion: 5 minutes

- Ask the girls the following questions:
  * What feelings did this conversation provoke?
  * How do you feel about your level of gossiping?
  * Did our discussion raise your awareness of the power of gossip and what it is used for?

Evaluation:

- Observe the girls participation and self-disclosure during conversation.

Homework:

- Journal Writing
  * In Salvaging Sisterhood today we...
  * How do you feel when people gossip about you?
  * When do you think gossip and rumors go too far?
  * FESS UP!

© YouthLight, Inc.

Digital Gossip

LESSON 5: GIRL TALK

Time: 45 minutes

Objectives:

* Girls will consider how destructive gossiping is on social media.
* Girls will learn to identify ways they take part in gossiping on social media.

Materials:

* Notebook paper
* Writing utensil
* "Declaration to Myself" cards

Opening: 5 minutes

* Journal discussion from previous week

Activity: 35 minutes

* Ask the girls about personal experiences with gossiping on social media.
* Ask each girl to think about the last conversation they had on social media. Pair the girls up and have them physically write down what they would say to each other – back and forth. Instruct group members not to talk!
* After about ten minutes, discuss the following points:
  * Did you get tired of writing out the conversation?
  * Did you say something that was taken out of context?
  * Have you ever written anything you wish you could take back?
  * How much do you gossip through texting or social media?
  * Have you ever sent out a message to a lot of people that you regret? What happened?

© YouthLight, Inc.

Digital Gossip
continued

LESSON 5: GIRL TALK

- Imagine having to hand write everything you have sent the past week through digital media! How long would it take you? How much would you really send? Would you read it first and then think it might not be a good thing to send?
- Have each girl pick a "Declaration to Myself" card.
- Thank the girls for sharing.

Discussion: 5 minutes

- Ask the girls the following questions:
  - How did this activity raise your awareness of the power of gossip and how it can get out of hand through digital media?
  - What are some ways you can stop yourself from gossiping through digital media?

Evaluation:

- Observe the girls willingness to self-disclose and participate in the activity.
- Observe whether or not the girls realized how much harm digital media can do to each other.

Homework:

- Journal Writing
  - In Salvaging Sisterhood today we...
  - How do you feel when people gossip about you?
  - When do you think gossip and rumors go too far?
  - FESS UP!
- Challenge the girls to hand write every conversation they would have (on social media or through texting) with school friends for a week. This means no actual digital communication that is not school related. If the girls want to send a forward to ten people, tell them to hand write it – ten times! Challenge the girls to pay attention to how out of hand gossiping through digital media can be.

© YouthLight, Inc.

What's My Reputation?

LESSON 5: GIRL TALK

Time: 45 minutes

Objectives:

- Girls will self-disclose what they perceive to be their "reputation" with others.
- Girls will consider how their behaviors mold others perceptions of them.
- Girls will become aware of how damaging reputations can be.

Opening: 5 Minutes

- Journal discussion from previous week

Materials:

- "What's My Reputation?" Activity
- Writing utensils
- "Declaration to Myself" cards

Activity: 35 minutes

- Ask and allow discussion for the following questions.
    - What is a reputation?
    - Can a reputation be good?
    - What makes a reputation bad?
    - What events change a reputation?
    - Once you have a bad rep, can you get it back?
    - Can gossip ruin a reputation?
    - Is it fair for others to judge you before they know you?
- Hand out "What's My Reputation?" worksheet and work on them as a group. Listen closely to how much the girls self-disclose and if they ask for their friends help. Point out when they do this and discuss (they will ask).
- Have each girl pick a "Declaration to Myself" card.
- Thank the girls for sharing.

© YouthLight, Inc.

What's My Reputation?

continued

LESSON 5: GIRL TALK

Discussion: 5 minutes

- Ask the girls the following questions:
    - Would you change anything about your reputation?
    - What are some ways you can keep your reputation "positive" in the future?

Evaluation:

- Observe the girls participation level and self-disclosure during conversation.
- Observe whether or not the girls agree with one another.

Homework:

- Journal Writing
    - In Salvaging Sisterhood today we...
    - How do you feel when people gossip about you?
    - When do you think gossip and rumors go too far?
    - FESS UP!

What's My Reputation? Worksheet

LESSON 5: GIRL TALK

Directions: Your reputation, simply defined, is what other people think about you. It may be good, bad, or a little of both. Answer the following questions in one sentence.

❀ What do your best friends think about you?

❀ What happened to make them think that?

❀ Is it ❏ TRUE ❏ FALSE ❏ KINDA BOTH?
If it is false, what would have caused your friends to believe that?

❀ What do your peers think about you?

❀ What happened to make them think that?

❀ Is it ❏ TRUE ❏ FALSE ❏ KINDA BOTH?
If it is false, what would have caused your friends to believe that?

❀ What do your teachers think about you?

❀ What happened to make them think that?

❀ Is it ❏ TRUE ❏ FALSE ❏ KINDA BOTH?
If it is false, what would have caused your friends to believe that?

© YouthLight, Inc.

Whatever!

LESSON 5: GIRL TALK

Time: 45 minutes

Objectives:

- Girls will learn to recognize jealousy.
- Girls will learn how to handle their feelings of jealousy.
- Girls will learn how to confront each other when they feel jealous.

Materials:

- Worksheet "Am I Jealous?"
- Worksheet "Dealing with Jealousy"
- Writing utensil
- "Declaration to Myself" cards

Opening: 5 minutes

- Journal discussion from previous week

Activity: 35 minutes

- Explain to the girls the meaning of jealousy.
- Make sure they don't confuse jealousy (destructive emotion) with envy (preoccupied/wistful emotion).
- Ask each girl to give an example of a time they felt jealous. It can be jealousy of a sibling, friend, celebrity, boyfriend, etc. Try to get the girls to disclose jealousy within the group.
- Distribute "Am I Jealous?" worksheet to each girl and allow the girls about 5 minutes to complete it.
- Discuss the results of the test.
- Distribute "Dealing with Jealousy" to each girl and work on it together.
- Discuss the worksheet as you go through it.
- Have each girl pick a "Declaration to Myself" card.
- Thank the girls for sharing.

© YouthLight, Inc.

Whatever!
continued

LESSON 5: GIRL TALK

Discussion: 5 minutes

❀ Ask the girls the following questions:
  ❀ How can you recognize jealousy?
  ❀ How will you handle your feelings of jealousy in the future?

Evaluation:

❀ Observe and confront any silent girls, silence may indicate tension.
❀ Observe the level of personal disclosure among the girls – were they being honest or talking about other people being jealous of them?

Homework:

❀ Journal Writing
  ❀ In Salvaging Sisterhood today we...
  ❀ What are some ways you can keep your reputation positive?
  ❀ FESS UP!

Am I Jealous?

LESSON 5: GIRL TALK

Chances are you have been really jealous of another friend. It is OK, it will happen. However, if your feelings are very intense and you feel you cannot control them, it might be time to evaluate your thought process so you don't lose a good friend. Take this quiz and circle the best answer – count them all up at the end and score yourself.

Would you get mad if your friend went out to dinner with another friend and did not invite you?
❏ YES   ❏ NO

You're at a party and your friend ignores you all night. She is hanging out with the guy she likes and tells you she is sorry later in the evening, but still does not really talk to you. Would you get mad?
❏ YES   ❏ NO

You and your best friend try out for the soccer team, she makes it – you don't. Do you tell your friends that you are better than her?
❏ YES   ❏ NO

You find out that your friend is lab partners with your boyfriend. Would you constantly question what they did in science?
❏ YES   ❏ NO

You find out that your friend got a better grade on a Math quiz that YOU helped her study for! Do you feel like it is not fair?
❏ YES   ❏ NO

If you know your friend is online talking to another friend and you message her but she doesn't repond, do you confront her?
❏ YES   ❏ NO

© YouthLight, Inc.

Am I Jealous?
continued

LESSON 5: GIRL TALK

If your friend does not call or text you back within an hour, do you keep calling her until she answers?

❏ YES ❏ NO

Do you get jealous if your friends have a secret that you don't know about?

❏ YES ❏ NO

You and your best friend have a sleepover and she talks on the phone all night with another friend. Would you be upset with her?

❏ YES ❏ NO

Have any of your friends ever told you that you are smothering them?

❏ YES ❏ NO

If you answered "Yes":

0-3 Times:
You rock! You know how to handle different situations and are obviously super secure with yourself. Keep it up.

4-6 Times:
You sometimes go a little overboard. Try to not let jealousy control your life because chances are, if you continue down this road, your feelings will start controlling your actions and you may see your friends disappearing one by one.

7-10 Times:
Girl, you need a reality check! If you keep this attitude up, you will soon have a real reason to be jealous – i.e., you will have no friends. People don't like to hang around someone that is always checking up on them – that is what their parents are there for. Talk to an adult about this and try to understand that while you are very important, everything is not about you. Ouch!

© YouthLight, Inc.

Dealing With Jealousy

LESSON 5: GIRL TALK

 Directions: Read each problem and solution. Discuss how you feel about the different scenarios with the group. When you are through, complete the bottom portion of the worksheet with the group.

Problem: You are hanging out exclusively with one girl in the group and others feel left out.

Friends can get super jealous when there is a third or fourth party involved, especially when someone is left out. This causes feelings of insecurity. Your friend might be worried that she will have nobody to chill with and then all of a sudden, they are mad at you! What can you do?

Solution: Don't put up a fight. Try to see eye to eye and understand that it is not fun to feel lonely and left out. If you need some space, tell her, but tell her nicely. It is OK to have more than one friend and sometimes everyone needs to branch out. Hang in there and openly communicate with each other.

Problem: You have a new boyfriend and are hanging out with him 24/7. If you are not with him, you are talking about him!

Boyfriends can cause major jealousy, especially if you are the only one in the group that has one. Your friends may feel like you like him more than them. Your friends might feel left out, jealous, and could try to ruin your relationship. Yikes!

Solution: When you are with your friends, focus only on them. Ask them how life is going, what's new, and do fun things together! Go shopping, paint your nails, have a sleepover, and have the same long talks you did before! Talk about your boyfriend, but don't smother your friends talking about him. If you are still having trouble, help them understand that you are having trouble too – it's hard to juggle school, activities, friends, and a new guy.

© YouthLight, Inc.

Dealing With Jealousy
continued

LESSON 5: GIRL TALK

Problem: You have a new friend in school that your friends don't like.

Your friends may think they will be replaced by her.

Solution: Assure your friends that they are still your friends. Introduce them to your new friend. Do something together that everyone likes.

Sometimes jealousy can get out of hand. If the following things start to happen maybe it is time to have a talk with your friend. Most likely, she does not even realize what she is doing. If you feel uncomfortable having this conversation with her, have an adult present (like your school counselor, teacher, or a parent) when you confront her.

- ❊ Your friend is constantly texting you and you are getting really annoyed.

- ❊ Your friend knows your social media passwords and is pretending to be you.

- ❊ Your friend comes over all the time, unannounced, and won't take the hint to leave.

- ❊ Your friend gets mad when you don't immediately reply to her texts.

- ❊ You feel smothered and are starting to dislike your friend.

© YouthLight, Inc.

Dealing With Jealousy
continued

LESSON 5: GIRL TALK

 We have talked about when your friends are jealous of you; but what about when you get jealous of them? What happenes when you are on the outs? Using what you have learned, try to list three possible situations when you might be jealous of your friends and then come up with possible solutions.

Problem: _____
_____
_____

Solution: _____
_____
_____
_____

Problem: _____
_____
_____

Solution: _____
_____
_____
_____

Problem: _____
_____
_____

Solution: _____
_____
_____

I'm Sorry, So Sorry!

LESSON 6: EMPATHY

Time: 45 minutes

Objectives:

- Girls will learn to admit mistakes.
- Girls will learn how to apologize.
- Girls will practice empathy.

Materials:

- Worksheet "The 5A Way to Make Everything OK"
- Poster board
- Writing materials – pencils, crayons, markers, and/or colored pencils
- "Declaration to Myself" cards

Opening: 5 minutes

- Journal discussion from previous week

Activity: 35 minutes

- Hand out the worksheet "The 5A Way to Make Everything OK" and follow the instructions on the worksheet.
- Distribute the art materials.
- Ask the girls to design a poster using the 5A Way.
- While drawing, ask the girls to share a time when their feelings were hurt by a friend. After each response, generate a discussion about how each situation was mended.
- When the girls are finished, hang the poster in your office or in the hallway.
- Have each girl pick a "Declaration to Myself" card.
- Thank the girls for sharing.

I'm Sorry, So Sorry!
continued

LESSON 6: EMPATHY

Discussion: 5 minutes

- Ask the girls the following questions:
    - How did it feel talking about a time you were hurt?
    - How could you apologize using the 5A method in the future?

Evaluation:

- Observe and confront any silent girls, silence may indicate tension.
- Observe the body language of the girls while discussing personal situations.

Homework:

- Journal Writing
    - In Salvaging Sisterhood today we...
    - When do you feel empathy toward other girls?
    - Why are girls supposed to be "nice" all of the time?
    - FESS UP!

The 5A Way to Make Everything OK

LESSON 6: EMPATHY

Directions: Choose two girls to act out the following role play and discuss the questions following the role play.

Jesse was caught cheating on her science test and is in serious trouble. Her parents are mad at her, her science teacher does not trust her anymore, and her best friend, Rhonda, won't talk to her because she was accused of letting Jesse cheat. Even though Jesse told the principal that Rhonda had no idea that she had cheated off of her test, Rhonda is still mad. Jesse was up really late and forgot to study and at first did not see the big deal; it was just a stupid science test! After a few days, she realized what a big mistake she made. Rhonda still won't sit next to her in any of her classes and is still really mad.

- What would you do if this situation happened to you?
- Could you ever forgive your friend if she cheated off of your paper?
- Could you ever apologize if you were the one caught?
- Would you be sorry if you didn't get caught? Why or why not?
- Demonstrate how Jesse should apologize to Rhonda.

Let's learn "The 5A Way to Make Everything OK!"

1. **Accept** that you made a mistake, it's OK – we all do!
2. **Admit** to your friend that you are responsible.
3. **Ask** to speak to your friend alone when there will be no interruption.
4. **Apologize** to your friend for hurting her feelings.
5. **Affirm** your friendship.

Now, using the 5A Method, how could Jesse apologize to Rhonda?

Next, creatively design "The 5A Way to Make Everything OK" poster. When you are finished, hang it up somewhere that you can look at it in case you forget.

When you are drawing, discuss times when you have been hurt or hurt somebody else and had to apologize. Using the "5A Way," how could you apologize differently?

© YouthLight, Inc.

But I Really DO Feel Bad!

LESSON 6: EMPATHY

Time: 45 minutes

Objectives:

- Girls will learn about empathy.
- Girls will practice using empathy.

Materials:

- "Guess How I Am Feeling" worksheet
- "Declaration to Myself" cards

Opening: 5 minutes

- Journal discussion from previous week

Activity: 35 minutes

- Ask the girls to explain what empathy is and ask for examples.
- Explain to the girls that empathy is the ability to understand what others are experiencing – walking a mile in their shoes.
- Read the situations below and discuss each with the girls.
- How would you feel if:
  - You are adopted and at school someone keeps making fun of you, saying your parents do not want you.
  - Your parents are getting a divorce and all of your friends' parents are married and seem to be happy. At school they are having a lunch for parents. Your parents don't get along and won't go if the other one is going.
  - Someone makes fun of you everyday about things you cannot help.
  - You just moved to a new school and nobody is friendly in the cafeteria. You ask to sit with a group of girls and they say, "No way," and laugh at you. You have to skip lunch or eat in the bathroom stall because you do not have anyone to sit with.
  - Your best friend turned against you because of an untrue rumor that you did not even start.

© YouthLight, Inc.

But I Really DO Feel Bad!

LESSON 6: EMPATHY

- You have a learning disability and everyone makes fun of you.
- Your parents can not afford to buy you new clothes and people call you "poor."
- You just found out that a girl in your class has cancer. You have been kind of mean to her and now you don't know how to act toward her.

* Give each girl a copy of "Guess How I Am Feeling."
* Pair each girl up.
* Have each girl pick a feeling and act it out. She can tell a story, mimic it in her body language, etc. Have their partner guess the feeling she is acting.
* Have a discussion about how body language affects feelings.
* Collect the feelings worksheet for next week's activity.
* Have each girl pick a "Declaration to Myself" card.
* Thank the girls for sharing.

Discussion: 5 minutes

* Ask the girls the following questions:
    - What does empathy mean?
    - How can you empathize with other people and their specific situations?

Evaluation:

* Observe the level of participation during group discussion.
* Observe the level of interaction during the role-plays. Were the girls serious or acting up?
* Observe whether or not the girls "guessed" correctly what their partner was feeling during the role plays.

Homework:

* Journal Writing
    - In Salvaging Sisterhood today we...
    - When do you feel empathy for other girls?
    - Why are girls supposed to be "nice" all of the time?
    - FESS UP!

© YouthLight, Inc.

Guess How I Am Feeling

LESSON 6: EMPATHY

Happy	**Miserable**	**Calm**
Excited	**Tearful**	**Content**
Eager	**Fidgety**	**Satisfied**
Joyful	**Anxious**	**Proud**
Shy	**Tense**	**Relaxed**
Bashful	**Worried**	**Surprised**
Helpless	**Restless**	**Startled**
Lonely	**Irritated**	**Afraid**
Unsure	**Mad**	**Shocked**
Confused	**Angry**	**Terrified**
Puzzled	**Upset**	**Safe**
Mixed-Up	**Furious**	**Secure**
Distracted	**Fearful**	**Confident**
Tired	**Embarrassed**	**Hopeful**
Sad	**Guilty**	**Trusting**
Down	**Self-Conscious**	**On Top of the WORLD**
Gloomy	**Ashamed**	

# Spreading Sunshine

LESSON 6: EMPATHY

Time: 45 minutes

Objectives:

- Girls will learn about kindness to others.
- Girls will practice sharing acts of kindness.

Opening: 5 minutes

- Journal discussion from previous week

Materials:

- Spreading Sunshine Cards – cut out and placed face down on the table
- 7 index cards for each girl
- Poster board and art materials (glue, glitter, markers, paint, pencils, etc.)
- "Declaration to Myself" cards

Activity: 35 minutes

- Ask the girls to discuss the meaning of kindness.
- Try to generate a discussion about specific, planned kindness and random acts of kindness.
- Ask the girls for examples of kindness.
- Ask the girls for examples of kindness from others. See if you can get specific feelings from the girls.
- Hand out poster board and art materials and have the girls create a "Kindness Creed." This can be a poem, a rap, a song, or a mantra that they believe they can follow to be kind to each other and those around them. If they are having trouble, spell out the word "KINDNESS" and have them make up a sentence for the beginning of each letter.
- When the girls are finished, hand them each a "Spreading Sunshine" card and 7 index cards.

Spreading Sunshine

LESSON 6: EMPATHY

- Explain to the girls that for a week they have to do one kind thing a day and not tell anyone! They must write it down on their index card and bring it to *Salvaging Sisterhood* next week. Each girl will get one "Sunshine Card" to start them off, but don't have to use it if they have another idea.
- Have each girl pick a "Declaration to Myself" card.
- Thank the girls for sharing.

Discussion – 5 minutes

- Ask the girls the following questions:
  - How do you feel about being kind and not telling other people?
  - Do you think the homework is going to be hard? Why or why not?
  - How will you follow the creed with your friends?
  - How will you follow the creed with other people?

Evaluation:

- Did the girls take the lesson seriously?
- Did the girls have a hard time coming up with a creed?
- Do the girls seem interested in the homework activity?

Homework:

- Spreading Sunshine Activity
- Journal Writing
  - In Salvaging Sisterhood today we...
  - When do you feel empathy toward other girls?
  - Why are girls supposed to be "nice" all of the time?
  - FESS UP!

Spreading Sunshine Cards

LESSON 6: EMPATHY

Smile at a stranger!	**Tell a cafeteria worker "thank you" for their hard work!**
Sit next to a different person at lunch!	**Pick up, and throw away, a piece of trash in the hallway!**
Hold a door open for the person behind you!	**Tell your Mom you like her outfit one morning!**
Give a compliment to a girl you never talk to!	**Offer to help your teacher clean up the classroom after school!**
Invite someone new to sit with your group at lunch!	**Apologize to someone whose feelings you once hurt!**
Have a conversation with three people you don't know!	**Sit next to a different person on the bus!**

© YouthLight, Inc.

Say What?

LESSON 7: COMMUNICATION & CONFRONTATION

Time: 45 minutes

Objectives:

- Girls will learn how to be more assertive and to constructively use "I" messages to express their feelings.
- Girls will learn to listen to each other by paraphrasing.

Opening: 5 minutes

- Journal discussion from previous week

Materials:

- "Guess How I Am Feeling" worksheet from previous week
- "I" Messages worksheet
- Writing utensil
- "Declaration to Myself" cards

Activity: 35 minutes

- Have the girls reflect on the group so far. Review the past topics. Explain to the girls that we have learned thus far about feelings and have become more aware of the negative ways we sometimes act.
- Explain to the girls what an "I" message is – an effective way to communicate what we feel, want, and/or need. Tell the girls that "I" messages are not a way to place blame, but to talk about how they feel.
- Give girls a few examples of "I" messages.
- Hand back the "Guess How I Am Feeling" worksheet and "I" Messages worksheet.
- Have each girl complete the worksheet, using examples from previous discussions and/or role plays.
- Discuss appropriate vs. inappropriate times to use "I" messages.
- Have each girl pick a "Declaration to Myself" card.
- Thank the girls for sharing.

© YouthLight, Inc.

Say What?
continued

LESSON 7: COMMUNICATION & CONFRONTATION

Discussion: 5 minutes

- Ask the girls the following questions:
    - Did anyone feel uncomfortable confronting each other?
    - How could you use an "I" message to a friend who hurt your feelings?

Evaluation:

- Did the girls listen to each other or make fun of each other when using the "I" messages?
- Were the girls able to correctly use the "I" messages?
- Do the girls know when and when not to use "I" messages?

Homework:

- Journal Writing
    - In Salvaging Sisterhood today we...
    - When do you feel comfortable standing up for yourself?
    - Is it hard to apologize when you are wrong?
    - Have you ever apologized when you did not do anything, just to make the problem go away?
    - FESS UP!

© YouthLight, Inc.

"I" Messages

LESSON 7: COMMUNICATION & CONFRONTATION

 "I" messages are cool because you say exactly how you feel! Nobody can tell you how you should feel. Now, let's practice using them.

You must ALWAYS begin with saying "I." Not you, me, she, he, etc. REMEMBER, by saying "I" – you avoid blaming.

After the "I," state your feeling (you can use your feeling worksheet if you need help with a word).

"I feel _____."

❋ **Next, tell the person *what* made you feel that way.**

"I feel _____, because _____."
OR
"I feel _____, when _____."

❋ **NOW – tell the person *why* you feel that way.**

"I feel _____, when you _____,

BECAUSE _____."

❋ **FINALLY, after the "I" message tell the person *what* you want.**

"I feel _____, when you _____,

BECAUSE _____."

AND "I want you to _____."

OR "I need you to _____."

Practice this everywhere. With your siblings, parents, teachers and friends. It is a great way to talk about your feelings without gossiping or getting angry, which can lead to a serious implosion!

© YouthLight, Inc.

Listen To Me!

LESSON 7: COMMUNICATION & CONFRONTATION

Time: 45 minutes

Objectives:

- Girls will learn to listen more effectively.
- Girls will learn to take turns talking and when to appropriately "chime" in.

Opening: 5 minutes

- Journal discussion from previous week

Materials:

- Bandanas for blindfolds (one for each member)
- "Declaration to Myself" cards

Activity: 35 minutes

- Explain to the girls the importance of listening to one another.
- Tell the girls they are going to have a conversation without using their eyes.
- Place a blindfold on each girl.
- Tell the girls that only one person can speak at a time.
- Allow the girls to pick a topic to discuss. If they are having trouble coming up with a topic, use one of "The Ties That Bind Us Questions" (page 27-29).
- Have the girls carry on a conversation for at least 20 minutes.
- Have each girl pick a "Declaration to Myself" card.
- Thank the girls for sharing.

© YouthLight, Inc.

Listen To Me!
continued

LESSON 7: COMMUNICATION & CONFRONTATION

Discussion: 5 minutes

- Ask the girls the following questions:
  - How did you feel not using your eyes?
  - Was it difficult to know when to speak?
  - Did you feel like others were listening to you?

Evaluation:

- Did the girls seem bored?
- Did the girls argue?
- Were the girls able to empathize with one another if appropriate?

Homework:

- Journal Writing
  - In Salvaging Sisterhood today we...
  - When do you feel comfortable standing up for yourself?
  - Is it hard to apologize when you are wrong?
  - Have you ever apologized when you did not do anything, just to make the problem go away?
  - FESS UP!

Problem Solving

LESSON 7: COMMUNICATION & CONFRONTATION

Time: 45 minutes

Objectives:

* Girls will learn strategies to effectively solve their friendship problems.
* Girls will learn to value their own opinions.

Opening: 5 minutes

* Journal discussion from previous week

Materials:

* "Problem Solving" worksheet
* "An Agreement to Disagree" worksheet
* Writing utensil
* "Declaration to Myself" cards

Activity: 35 minutes

* Have the girls reflect on the group so far. Review the past topics. Talk to the group members about what they have learned thus far about feelings.
* Ask the girls how they usually solve their friendship problems. Give a general example if needed, such as, if someone is mad at another girl for not talking to her during lunch, how would they work it out?
* Hand out the "Problem Solving" worksheet.
* Have the girls come to a consensus about a problem that has occurred between them.
* Have each girl work quietly on the worksheet.
* When all of the girls have completed the worksheet, have them share their problem solving techniques with the group.
* Discuss the fact that there is no "right or wrong" way to solve a problem, as long as it is solved.
* Distribute "An Agreement to Disagree" to each girl.

© YouthLight, Inc.

Problem Solving
continued

LESSON 7: COMMUNICATION & CONFRONTATION

- ❀ Go over the worksheet with them and make extra copies available as needed.
- ❀ Have each girl pick a "Declaration to Myself" card.
- ❀ Thank the girls for sharing!

Discussion: 5 minutes

- ❀ Ask the girls the following questions:
  - ❋ Did anyone feel uncomfortable sharing their thoughts on the problem?
  - ❋ Did anyone disagree?
  - ❋ Is it OK to disagree?
  - ❋ How can you use "Problem Solving" in the future to help your friendship problems?

Evaluation:

- ❀ Did the girls get upset with one another?
- ❀ Were the girls able to correctly use the problem solving method?
- ❀ Did the girls catch on quickly and seem like they could use it without the help of an adult?
- ❀ Did the girls think it is OK to not always agree with their friends?

Homework:

- ❀ Journal Writing
  - ❋ In Salvaging Sisterhood today we...
  - ❋ When do you feel comfortable standing up for yourself?
  - ❋ Is it hard to apologize when you are wrong?
  - ❋ Have you ever apologized when you did not do anything, just to make the problem go away?
  - ❋ FESS UP!

Problem Solving Worksheet

LESSON 7: COMMUNICATION & CONFRONTATION

So, you have this huge issue with your friend that is taking over your life. It needs to be solved right now! Think of a recent issue that you had with a friend. Summarize it in the space provided below. Next, follow the seven steps in this worksheet to figure out and fix your friendship woes. Pretty soon, you are going to be a problem solving expert!

What's the general problem?

_____
_____
_____

❈ STEP ONE
What is the underlying concern? What are you most angry or upset about? You have to know what is wrong in order to work towards a solution.
My concern is:_____
_____
_____

❈ STEP TWO
Where/when did the concern begin? It is important to know how it started to work towards a solution.
My concern began when: _____
_____
_____

❈ STEP THREE
What have you already tried to help solve it? You need to figure out what will and won't work to help the problem.
To help the situation, I have tried to:_____
_____
_____
_____

© YouthLight, Inc.

Problem Solving Worksheet continued

LESSON 7: COMMUNICATION & CONFRONTATION

❀ STEP FOUR
What do you want the outcome to be? You should have a goal in mind when trying to resolve an issue.
I want: _____
_____
_____

❀ STEP FIVE
What are some possible barriers? If you could hit a bump in the road, it is important to know ahead of time.
Possible barriers are: _____
_____
_____

❀ STEP SIX
What else could you do? We always need alternatives just in case it does not go as planned (AKA – plan B, C, D, E:)
These are other options to help resolve the issue: _____
_____
_____

❀ STEP SEVEN
How did it go? If it is not how you wanted it to be, what is the compromise or what will you try next? You should always evaluate your steps to help you in the future.
This is what happened: _____
_____
_____

❀ NEXT, I WILL TRY: _____
_____
_____

An Agreement to Disagree

LESSON 7: COMMUNICATION & CONFRONTATION

It's OK if you don't always agree with your friends. Nobody is alike and we all have different opinions. When you don't agree with your friends, here are some things you can say to them (instead of "you are so wrong!")

- I understand where you are coming from.
- I admire your passion.
- I appreciate your viewpoint.
- There's a fresh perspective!
- I can see you have really thought about this.
- I appreciate your insight, or...
- Wow, what a cool point!

Never say the word, "*BUT*." That word usually puts people on the defense, kind of like you don't really care what they think. For example, if you said to your friend after an argument, "Now I get where you are coming from, BUT, I am still right."

If you still disagree and cannot see eye to eye, it might be time to "Agree to Disagree." Below is a sample contract – see if you can make a really cool one and put it in your journal in case of emergency.

❀ ❀ ❀ ❀ ❀ ❀

I, _____, agree to disagree with _____. We both have excellent opinions and neither one of us is wrong! We refuse to fight about this, or bring our other friends in on it because we are both entitled to our own thoughts.

Signature _____

Signature _____

Date _____

© YouthLight, Inc.

Sisters Forever

LESSON 8: SISTERS FOREVER

Time: 45 minutes

Objectives:

* Girls will demonstrate an understanding of what they learned in group.
* Girls will sign a contract agreeing to effectively solve future "friend" woes.
* Girls will evaluate the *Salvaging Sisterhood* group.

Opening: 5 minutes

* Journal discussion from previous week

Materials:

* Snack of choice
* "Dear *Salvaging Sisterhood* Friendship Expert" worksheet for each girl.
* "*Salvaging Sisterhood* Contract" for each girl.
* "*Salvaging Sisterhood* Group Evaluation" for each girl.

Activity: 35 minutes

* Give each girl a copy of "Dear *Salvaging Sisterhood* Friendship Expert."
* Hand out the snack.
* One at a time, have a girl read a situation.
* Have the girls discuss what they would do in each situation.
* Hand out "*Salvaging Sisterhood* Contract" to each girl.
* Go over the contract and have each girl autograph one another's.
* Hand out an evaluation for each girl to complete.

© YouthLight, Inc.

Sisters Forever
continued

LESSON 8: SISTERS FOREVER

Discussion: 5 minutes

❈ Ask each girl to talk about their favorite part of *Salvaging Sisterhood* and how they will use what they have learned in the future.

Evaluation:

❈ Did girls actively apply what they learned in group during the "Dear Salvaging Sisterhood Friendship Expert" discussion?
❈ Did all of the girls agree to the contract with ease?

Follow-up:

❈ In 4-6 weeks check in with each girl to assess their progress by both verbal communication and post-group evaluation.
❈ Optional Journal Writing:
  ❈ I learned a lot of things in *Salvaging Sisterhood* about myself including:
  ❈ What is the most important thing you learned in group?
  ❈ How are you going to use what you learned in the future?

Dear Salvaging Sisterhood Friendship Expert

LESSON 8: SISTERS FOREVER

 Below you will find a bunch of scenarios that girls endure daily. Using what you have learned in *Salvaging Sisterhood*, how would you handle each situation?

I have been best friends with Jessica since the fourth grade. Now that we are in middle school things have been kind of rocky. She is hanging out with more popular girls and I think she is ignoring me. At lunch I sit with her and her friends make fun of me and tell me they are kidding when I get mad. This guy sits with us that I can't stand and one day he put ketchup in my chair and Jessica laughed so hard she was crying. He ruined my new pants and she told me to get over it. I don't know what to do!

My friend Tala has been my best friend since second grade. We are now in the sixth grade and still good friends, but she has started hanging out with other girls and is acting like she is too good for me and is talking behind my back. This upsets me because I feel like she abandoned me for them. This summer my family went on vacation and I brought Tala with me. We have so much fun when we are not in school. I introduced Tala to my friend Karen and now they hang out with each other and leave me out and I am the one who made them hang out in the first place. What should I do?

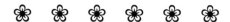

My friends always talk about people behind their backs. I do admit that I join in, but they are so mean sometimes and it gets out of control. I want them to stop because some of the things they say are about my friends, are racist, or about people with disabilities. Should I tell them to stop and risk them talking about me?

Dear Salvaging Sisterhood Friendship Expert *continued*

LESSON 8: SISTERS FOREVER

I have a problem with jealousy. I have never told anyone this before but I feel like my friends have everything that I don't and I try to get back at them. Like I talk to my friend's boyfriend on social media all the time and lie to him about her to break them up. I know their email passwords and check to make sure they are not talking about me. I have even deleted messages from other people and used their names to gossip! I hate that I do this but I always have to know everything. It is not fair to them and I am afraid if I keep doing it they will find out and I will lose everyone! HELP!

My best friend is getting annoying. I can't breathe because she is smothering me. She always wants to hang out and gets super mad if I even talk to other people. And she like does things like leaves notes in my locker and once she even showed up at the grocery store with her Mom when I told her I had to go there with my Mom! I like hanging out with her but I sometimes need space. What should I tell her?

My best friend came up to me and said that I can't hang out with her for two weeks because she wants to hang out with other people, but in two weeks she will be ready to hang out with me again. I like can't go two weeks and this is not fair but there is nothing I can do. She said we can text and message each other. I think this is wrong! Am I being hypersensitive?

My friends have been excluding me lately and when they do, they talk about it in front of me. Like yesterday, they were talking about how they went to dinner at this nice restaurant with Madison's family and how fun it was. Last week they all went to the pool without me and totally rubbed it in my face. This is so not cool and I always come home and cry. My mom says I should find new friends but I don't want to. Should I keep dealing with it?

© YouthLight, Inc.

Dear Salvaging Sisterhood Friendship Expert continued

LESSON 8: SISTERS FOREVER

I wanted to have a party on Saturday but when I told my friends they said they could not come because of different reasons. I was like "OK" and changed it for next month. So get this, I just got an invite to my friend's party and it is Saturday. All of my friends said they got out of their "commitments." That's cool and all, but how come they ditched everyone for her and not me? I don't even want to have mine now because I am so hurt. Should I still have it? Should I go to my friend's house on Saturday?

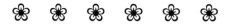

My so-called "best friend" always does things like hits me and smacks me and yells really loud at me. If I even jokingly poke her, she cries. She always tells me that I am her only friend that she can trust and that she would not come to school if we were not friends. But I can't take this anymore and I have asked her to stop. Sometimes I want to punch her so hard her glasses fall off her face.

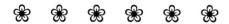

There is this new girl in school who is taking all of my friends and she does not like me. I am afraid she is stealing my spotlight and I want her to stop. How do I make my friends stop hanging out with her and start hanging out with me again?

Friendship First Aid

LESSON 8: SISTERS FOREVER

Time: 45 minutes

Objectives:

- Girls will demonstrate an understanding of what they learned in group.
- Girls will discuss how to effectively solve future "friend" woes.
- Girls will evaluate the *Salvaging Sisterhood* group.

Opening: 5 minutes

- Journal discussion from previous week

Materials:

- Snack of choice
- A shoebox, cardboard box, or brown lunch bag for each girl
- "Friendship First Aid Kit" worksheet for each girl.
- Various first aid kit items (listed on supplemental worksheet)
- Art materials (glitter, markers, etc.)
- "*Salvaging Sisterhood* Post-Group Survey" for each girl.
- Certificate acknowledging completion of *Salvaging Sisterhood* for each girl.

Activity: 35 minutes

- Hand out the snack.
- Put the box in the middle of the table and explain to the girls they are going to design a "Friendship First Aid Kit."
- Hand out the "Friendship First Aid Kit" worksheet.
- Hand out the art materials and have the girls decorate their box or bag.
- Put the first aid items on the table and read each one while simultaneously giving each girl the item to place in her bag.
- Remind girls of the "*Salvaging Sisterhood* contract" they have signed.

© YouthLight, Inc.

Friendship First Aid
continued

LESSON 8: SISTERS FOREVER

- Hand out post-survey for each girl to complete.
- Provide each girl a certificate of completion.
- Thank girls for participating in group and tell them you will be following up with each of them at a later date.

Discussion: 5 minutes

- Ask each girl to say what their favorite part of *Salvaging Sisterhood* was and how they will use what they have learned in the future.

Evaluation:

- Did girls enjoy making the "Friendship First Aid Kit?"
- Did the girls understand the meaning of the items in the kit?

Follow-up:

- In 4-6 weeks check in with each girl to assess their progress by both verbal communication and post-group evaluation.
- Optional Journal Writing:
  - I learned a lot of things in *Salvaging Sisterhood* about myself including:
  - What is the most important thing you learned in group?
  - How are you going to use what you learned in the future?

LESSON 8: SISTERS FOREVER

Friendship First Aid Kit

Tissues to dry our tears

Band-Aids to heal our hurt feelings

Hershey Hugs and Kisses to help us make-up with each other

An eraser to remind us that it's OK to make mistakes

A piece of yarn to tie our friendship together

A penny to bring our friendship good luck

A pack of sugar to sweeten up bitterness

Gum to help us stick together

Paper to write down our feelings

A piece of chalk to remind us that sometimes we have to "chalk it up!"

A star sticker to remind us to shine

A toothpick to remind us to pick our battles

A lifesaver to remind us that we will ALWAYS be there for each other

Salvaging Sisterhood Contract

LESSON 8: SISTERS FOREVER

From now on we will:.

Talk about our problems to each other.

Use "I Messages" to express how we feel.

Take responsibility for our actions.

Not spread rumors about each other.

Not be jealous of each other and cherish our differences.

Talk about solving the problem instead of being the problem.

Stick together and be role models for girls everywhere.

Not use our friendship against one another.

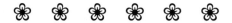

Salvaging Sisterhood Autographs

© YouthLight, Inc.

Salvaging Sisterhood Group Evaluation

LESSON 8: SISTERS FOREVER

Did you learn anything from this *Salvaging Sisterhood*? ❏ YES ❏ NO
If yes, what? _____
_____

Were the *Salvaging Sisterhood* topics useful? ❏ YES ❏ NO

The most helpful part of *Salvaging Sisterhood* was _____
_____

The least helpful part of *Salvaging Sisterhood* was _____
_____

Did you feel comfortable in *Salvaging Sisterhood*? ❏ YES ❏ NO
If no, why? _____
_____

Did you like journaling? ❏ YES ❏ NO

Was the *Salvaging Sisterhood* adult leader helpful? ❏ YES ❏ NO

Would you recommend *Salvaging Sisterhood* to your friends? ❏ YES ❏ NO

Overall *Salvaging Sisterhood* was:
❏ BORING   ❏ OK   ❏ SUPER FUN

© YouthLight, Inc.

Salvaging Sisterhood Post-Group Survey

LESSON 8: SISTERS FOREVER

Directions: Please take a few moments to answer (HONESTLY) these questions! Only circle one answer unless otherwise indicated!

1. Do you know a lot of "little details" about your friends? For example, their birthday, favorite color, how many brothers/sisters they have, their favorite food, etc.?
   - ❑ Of course I do.
   - ❑ A few things.
   - ❑ Um, no.

2. Do your friends know a lot about you?
   - ❑ Of course they do.
   - ❑ A few things.
   - ❑ No way.

3. Since *Salvaging Sisterhood* began, do you say things to your friends that are kind of mean, but then say "just kidding" or "SIKE" – but you really mean it?
   - ❑ Yes
   - ❑ No
   - ❑ Sometimes

4. Since *Salvaging Sisterhood* began, if you hear some juicy news (true or not) about a friend do you: (Check only one)
   - ❑ Keep it to yourself and not tell a soul, no matter what.
   - ❑ Just tell your best friend and make her PROMISE not to tell anyone.
   - ❑ Tell just the people you think should know.
   - ❑ Tell everyone.

5. Would you stay home from a sleepover, party, movies, etc. if your friend was having a bad day and really needed to talk to you?
   - ❑ Always.
   - ❑ It depends.
   - ❑ No way, her problem will be there when I am done.

6. If you are having a problem with a friend, check two ways you would deal with it:
   - ❑ Tell her.
   - ❑ Tell a friend.
   - ❑ Text her.
   - ❑ Email her.
   - ❑ Ask everyone if she is mad at me.
   - ❑ Make up a rumor about her.
   - ❑ Don't invite her to a social gathering.
   - ❑ Ignore it and hope it will go away.

© YouthLight, Inc.

Congratulations!

_____
Name

_____
Date

You Have Successfully Completed Our Group and Now Have the Tools to Salvage Sisterhood! Use Them Everyday and Keep up the Terrific Work!

_____
Group Leader Signature

To the Parent/Guardian of _____:

    This letter is to thank you for allowing your daughter to participate in *Salvaging Sisterhood*! We had a lot of fun and your daughter learned important skills to communicate more effectively with her friends. We have completed the group, but I will be periodically checking in on your daughter and her friends to review their progress. In a month or so, I will be giving the group a post-group evaluation and meeting with them to hear verbally how they are using what they learned in *Salvaging Sisterhood*!

Although *Salvaging Sisterhood* has ended, I am always here to help if you or your daughter has any concerns or comments. Please do not hesitate to contact me if you have any questions.

Sincerely,

Salvaging Sisterhood Group Leader

© YouthLight, Inc.

Salvaging Sisterhood Follow-up Questionnaire

HOW'S IT GOING _____?

This is just a follow-up to see how you and your friends have been doing since *"Salvaging Sisterhood"* ended. Please take a minute to tell me. When you are done, please put it in my mailbox.

* What do you remember from group?

* Do you use the skills that you learned in group?

* Do you still get along with your friends from group?

* Did you teach anybody else something that you learned in group?

* Do you still journal?

* Do you think your friendships are better as a result of group?

* Is there anything else you want to tell me?

© YouthLight, Inc.

Publications About Relational Aggression/Bullying

Casey-Cannon, S., Hayward, C., & Gowen, K. (2001). Middle-school girls' reports of peer victimization: Concerns, consequences, and implications. Professional School Counseling, 5(2), 138-147.

Craig, W. M., Henderson, K., & Murphy, J. G. (2000). Prospective teachers' attitudes toward bullying and victimization. School Psychology International, 21, 5-21.

Crick, N. R., Bigbee, M. A., & Howes, C. (1996). Gender differences in children's normative beliefs about aggression: How do I hurt thee? Let me count the ways. Child Development, 67, 1003-1014.

Crick, N. R., Casas, J. F., & Ku, H. (1999). Physical and relational peer victimization in pre-school. Developmental Psychology, 35, 376-385.

Crick, N. R., Casas, J. F., & Mosher, M. (1997). Relational and overt aggression in preschool. Developmental Psychology, 33, 579-588.

Crick, N. R., Casas, J. F., & Nelson, D. A. (2002). Toward a more comprehensive understanding of peer maltreatment: Studies of relational victimization. Current Directions in Psychological Science, 11(3), 98-101.

Crick, N. R., & Grotpeter, J. K. (1995). Relational aggression, gender, and social-psychological adjustment. Child Development, 66, 710-722.

Crick, N. R., & Grotpeter, J. K. (1996). Children's treatment by peers: Victims of relational and overt aggression. Development and Psychopathology, 8, 367-380.

Deak, J. (2002). Girls will be girls: Raising confident and courageous daughters. New York, NY: Hyperion.

Dellasega, C. & Nixon, C. (2003). Girl wars: 12 strategies that will end female bullying. New York, NY: Simon & Schuster.

Espelage, D. L., & Asidao, C. (2001). Interviews with middle school students: Bullying, victimization, and contextual variables. Journal of Emotional Abuse, 2, 49-62.

Espelage, D. L., & Holt, M. K. (2001). Bullying and victimization during early adolescence: Peer influences and psychosocial correlates. Journal of Emotional Abuse, 2, 123-142.

Galen, B., & Underwood, J. K. (1997). A developmental investigation of social aggression among children. Developmental Psychology, 33, 589-600.

Grotpeter, J. K., & Crick, N. R. (1996). Relational aggression, overt aggression, and friendship. Child Development, 67, 2328-2338.

Hennington, C., Hughes, J. N., Cavell, T. A., & Thompson, B. (1998). The role of relational aggression in identifying aggressive boys and girls. Journal of School Psychology, 36, 457-477.

Jeffrey, L. R., Miller, D., & Linn, M. (2001). Middle school bullying as a context for the development of passive observers to the victimization of others. Journal of Emotional Abuse, 2, 143-156.

Karnes, E. (2004). Mean chicks, cliques and dirty tricks. Avon, MA: Adams Media.

Publications About Relational Aggression/Bullying ...continued

Kupkovits, J. (2011). Relational aggression in girls: A prevention and intervention curriculum with activities and lessons for small groups and classrooms. Chapin, SC: YouthLight.

Pellegrini, A. D., Bartini, M., & Brooks, F. (1999). School bullies, victims, and aggressive victims: Factors relating top group affiliation and victimization in early adolescence. Journal of Educational Psychology, 91, 216-224.

Pipher, M. (1994). Reviving Ophelia. New York, NY: Ballentine.

Prinstein, M. J., Boergers, J., & Vernberg, E. M. (2001). Overt and relational aggression in adolescents: Social-psychological adjustment of aggressors and victims. Journal of Clinical Child Psychology, 30(4), 479-491.

Randall, K. & Bowen, A. (2011). Mean girls: 101 1/2 creative strategies and activities for working with relational aggression. Chapin, SC: YouthLight.

Roecker-Phelps, C. E. (2001). Children's responses to overt and relational aggression. Journal of Clinical and Child Psychology, 30, 240-252.

Salmivalli, C., Lagerspetz, K., Bjorkqvist, K., Osterman, K., & Kaukiainen, A. (1996). Bullying as a group process: Participant roles and their relations to social status within the group. Aggressive Behavior, 22, 1-15.

Savin-Williams, R. C., & Berndt, T. J. (1990). Friendship and peer relationships. In S. S. Feldman & G. R. Elliott (Eds.), At the threshold: The developing adolescent (pp. 277-307). Cambridge, MA: Harvard University Press.

Schwartz, D. & Kenny, K. (2008). Girls' clubs rock! A prevention approach for helping groups of teen girls navigate through the challenges of adolescence. Chapin, SC: YouthLight.

Simmons, R. (2002). Odd girl out: The hidden culture of aggression in girls. New York: Harcourt.

Swearer, S. M., & Doll, B. (2001). Bullying in schools: An ecological framework. Journal of Emotional Abuse, 2, 7-23.

Taylor-Greene, S., Brown, D., Nelson, L., Longton, J., Gassman, T., Cohen, J., et al. (1997). School-wide behavioral support: Starting the year off right. Journal of Behavioral Education, 7, 99-112.

Taylor, J.V. (November 2004). Middle Grade Madness, Debunking the Myth of the Queen Bee. *American School Counselor Magazine*. American School Counselor Association: Alexandria, VA

Underwood, M. K., Galen, B. R., & Paquette, J. A. (2001). Top ten challenges for understanding gender aggression in children: Why can't we all just get along? Social Development, 10, 248-266.

Werner, N. E., & Crick, N. R. (1999). Relational aggression and social psychological adjustment in a college sample. Journal of Abnormal Psychology, 108, 615-623.

Wiseman, R. (2002). Queen Bees and Wannabes: Helping Your Daughter Survive Cliques, Gossip, Boyfriends, and Other Realities of Adolescence. Three Rivers Press, NY, NY.

Yoon, J., & Kerber, K. (2003). Bullying: Elementary teachers' attitudes and intervention strategies. Research in Education, 69, 27-35.

References

Bartow, H. & Salkeld, S. (2001). *Challenging the Barbie doll syndrome: A group design for working with adolescent females.* Warminster, PA: Marco Products.

Bjoerkqvist, K., Lagerspetz, K. M. J., & Kaukianen, A. (1992). Do girls manipulate and boys fight? Developmental trends in regard to direct and indirect aggression. *Aggressive Behavior, 18*, 117-127.

Casey-Cannon, S., Hayward, C., & Cowen, K. (2001). Middle-school girls' reports of peer victimization: Concerns, consequences, and implications. *Professional School Counselor, (5)2*, 138-148.

Crick, N. R., & Grotpeter, J. K. (1995). Relational aggression, gender, and social-psychological adjustment. *Child Development, 66*, 710-722.

Crick, N. R., & Nelson, D. A. (2002). Relational and physical victimization within friendships: Nobody told me there'd be friends like these.Ê *Journal of Abnormal Child Psychology, 30*, 599-607.

Campbell, C.A., & Dahir, C.A. (1997). *Sharing the vision: The national standards for school counseling programs.* Alexandria, VA: American School Counselor Association.

Perlstein, D. (March, 2000). Failing at kindness: Why fear of violence endangers children. *Educational Leadership, 57*(6), 76-79.

Taylor, J.V. (November 2004). Middle Grade Madness, Debunking the myth of the queen bee. *American School Counselor Magazine.* American School Counselor Association: Alexandria, VA

The American School Counselor Association: Retrieved November 23rd, 2004 from http://www.schoolcounselor.org.

The Ophelia Project. (n.d.). *Researching relational aggression.* Retrieved December 7th, 2004 from http://www.opheliaproject.org.

Underwood, M. K. (2003). *Preventing and reducing social aggression among girls.* The Brown University Child and Adolescent Letter. Retrieved December 10th, 2004 from http://www.childresearch.net/CYBRARY/NEWS/200312.HTM.

Helpful Websites About Relational Aggression/Bullying

* Websites are subject to change.

Amy Poehler's Smart Girls at the Party
www.amysmartgirls.com

Girl Tips by Rachel Simmons
www.rachelsimmons.com/advice/girltips/

Rosalind Wiseman
www.rosalindwiseman.com

The Ophelia Project
www.opheliaproject.org

© YouthLight, Inc.